THE LIFE OF A
DANGEROUS
WITNESS
—— WITH ——
STUDY GUIDE

BY MIKE BAKER, TYLER HARI, J.K. JONES AND JIM PROBST
EDITED BY JIM PROBST

OPEN: The Life of a Dangerous Witness

ISBN 978-0-9841094-9-4

Published in 2013
by
College Press Publishing Co.
Printed and bound in the USA

TABLE OF CONTENTS

INTRODUCTION

This book began where many of the Holy Spirit's promptings begin with me these days, in fellowship with other Christians. A casual evening conversation with some of my best friends (who also happen to be co-pastors) turned into a discussion about how we could encourage Christ followers to be better at sharing their faith. A few Scriptures were quoted, some insights were given, and many ideas were shared. Before long, one word seemed to be impressed upon our hearts simultaneously. I love it when the Spirit does that! The word He gave us that cool October evening was the word "open."

If Christ followers are to become dangerous witnesses, (remember, "martyr" first meant "to give testimony" but came to mean "death" for that testimony—dangerous indeed!) then some things are going to have to open. The Scriptures and this study both encourage us to pray for, to look for, and to walk through openings to share the good news we have in Jesus. We need to be *open* to sharing our lives with outsiders. We need to *openly* share our stories of faith. We need to pray for the Spirit to *open* doors for us speak. And we need to *open* our mouths when the time is right.

This study tool is all about these series of openings that take place every time someone comes to know Jesus as Lord and Savior. But this book is also more than just a study. In an effort to help each of us find ourselves in the context of the bigger story, we have created a very unique book that addresses evangelism from several different angles. This book is a study. This book is a history. This book is a testimony. This book is a training manual. These all come together to help you prepare to share your faith.

What is the goal? Our prayer is that everyone who completes this study will be equipped and motivated to do one simple thing— become a disciple for Jesus. We believe that this goal is what Jesus called his followers to do in Matthew 28, and we believe it's the most important, eternal goal we can achieve. Prayerfully, in the months and years after this study, thousands will walk through the open door of faith in Christ and learn to live.

Mike Baker
Eastview Christian Church
May 2013

WEEK ONE

OPEN LIVES

MONDAY; A BIBLICAL PERSPECTIVE

"Your first and best witness is the life you live!"

"Preach the Gospel at all times and when necessary use words."
Attributed to Francis of Assisi

"But in your hearts set apart Christ as Lord. Always be prepared to give an answer to everyone who asks you to give the reason for the hope that you have. But do this with gentleness and respect..." I Peter 3:15 NIV

When I was a junior in high school, a speaker at a conference I attended challenged Christian students to live out their faith in visible ways. One tangible way he suggested was to carry a Bible to school along with all our other school supplies. This, he suggested, would show dependence on the written word of God and would open conversations with fellow class mates concerning Jesus. In response to his challenge, my friends and I committed to carrying our Bibles to school.

Looking back, saying "yes" to carrying my Bible openly was not much of a sacrifice, but I remember being nervous as I walked down the hall with a stack of books that included the Scriptures. Admittedly, I was scared, but I was also emboldened by the knowledge that I was not alone. My friends and I had committed to placing our Bibles on the front corner of our desks in every class we attended. We also committed to prayer before lunch in the school cafeteria (a prayer of thanks...and protection from really bad food).

Of course, by this time in my life, I was fully engaged in following God's calling to be a preacher. This path gave me the perfect answer when the questions inevitably came (which they did). When anyone asked me why I was carrying a Bible, I simply replied that I was going to be a preacher, so it was the most important book in my life. Most kids simply responded with an intelligent, "Oh" or "cool." Some actually said they were Christians and were glad I was carrying it. Others asked me about being a pastor and some theological questions.

Eventually, this Bible witness garnered me the nickname "Rev" that many classmates called me throughout the remainder of my high school years. For over a year and a half, I responded to "Rev" in the halls, the classroom, and at school events ("Tyrone" was my other nickname and another story entirely). After a while, it was not a big deal to carry my Bible or to be known as "Rev." But my witness and influence continued to define me, as I soon discovered.

Late in my final year of high school, I was sitting in the journalism room with five or six classmates, just hanging around. As a senior, I only had three required courses remaining, so I spent four hours of my day working as the sports editor of the school newspaper. It was in one of those bull sessions that a girl started telling a dirty joke. I was not in the group she was addressing, but I was within earshot, and, as she delivered the punch line, everyone broke into laughter...including me! Suddenly, all eyes were on me, and the girl who had told the joke hypocritically exclaimed, "Rev. you're not supposed to laugh at that!"

It was an astounding lesson for me concerning my witness that I have not forgotten to this day. As a follower of Jesus, your first and best witness is the life you live. You can carry your Bible to school. You can put a Christian bumper sticker on your car. You can wear Christian t-shirts, listen to Christian music, and pray before meals in public, but your greatest chance at sharing your faith comes from living a consistent Christian life. When your family, friends, co-workers, classmates, and neighbors see a life of faith in Jesus, they will be more likely to listen to what you have to say about Him.

In his first letter, Peter says that Christ-followers should always be ready to talk about their faith, which is what this "open" study is all about. In chapter three of his letter, Peter writes, "Always be prepared to give an answer to everyone who asks you to give the reason for the hope that you have" (I Peter 3:15). In other words, live an open life that reveals an inner faith and then be ready to talk about it. Over the course of this study, we will learn how to give an answer, how to explain the Christian faith, and how to talk about our individual journeys with Jesus, but all of this preparation will be useless if we don't live it. Three quick lessons from this passage tell us how our lives and witnesses work together.

Live a life of hope. When people look at your life, do they see hope or something else? The greatest witness for us is how we face life and its circumstances. Remember, people are watching our every move. They notice how we deal with setbacks. They see the faith we exhibit when someone we love is dealing with cancer or dies suddenly. They see our value system by watching how we prioritize our time, money, and passion. They watch us when everyone else is stressed, or frustrated, or afraid. If we are ever to influence our friends to have faith in Christ, they are first going to have to see the hope that Jesus has given us.

Always be prepared. You never know when it's going to happen. But if you live a life of faith, sooner or later those around you will want to ask you about it. Sometimes, the opening is simply a subtle comment like, "you know, I used to go to church as a kid." Other times, this conversation is driven by need ("You go to church don't you? Would you pray for my mom?...") or desperation ("Man, my life is a mess right now..."). Some just blurt out, "Are you a Christian?" while others inquire, "what's different about you?" All of these lines are opportunities to have conversations with someone about Jesus, and, since we don't know when these opportunities will happen, we must be prepared at all times. In traffic, in study hall, in play group, in the bleachers, in the restaurant, in between innings, in the back-yard, and on the street corner, these openings for faith conversations take place. Are you prepared?

Give an answer. The Greek word for "answer" in this verse is the word *apologia*. It is the word we get "apology" from, and it literally means "to give a verbal defense or argument." It was often used in the legal sense when a governing body interrogated someone. This definition is not an argument in the sense of being abrasive or argumentative. Remember, Peter reminds us to give this defending response for our hope with "gentleness and respect." Theologians often devote themselves to "apologetics" so that they have the ability to defend the faith and to give answers for questions regarding the Christian faith. But most of us won't require this deep kind of study. As Christians, we are not apologizing for something wrong with Christianity; we are simply giving an explanation for why only Jesus makes sense in our lives. Prayerfully, by the end of this study, you will be able to share your faith in a simple and engaging way, but you already know more than you think. The simple answer is Jesus. When someone sees a difference in us and asks us what it's all about, we can simply and honestly say, "my life is different because of Jesus." This is the first step to becoming a witness, and it all begins with the lives we live.

WEEK 1: TUESDAY;
AN HISTORICAL PERSPECTIVE

PETER
AN HISTORICAL PERSPECTIVE

Typically, when we think of an apostle (*apostolos* - "sent one"), we count twelve, not thirteen or fourteen. I trust, though, I will be able to persuade you that the number of apostles in the New Testament is far greater than twelve. Those of us who read the Bible, especially the Gospels, are aware of the first twelve Jesus called to be His disciples: Peter, Andrew, James son of Zebedee, John, Philip, Bartholomew (also called Nathanael), Thomas, Matthew (also called Levi), James son of Alphaeus, Thaddaeus (also called Judas, the brother of James), Simon the Zealot, and Judas Iscariot (Matthew 10:2-4; Mark 3:16-19; Luke 6:13-16; and Acts 1:13-26). Judas Iscariot, of course, sadly took his own life. The Jerusalem church, in response to that suicide, prayerfully selected Matthias to take his place (Acts 1:23). Apart from those individuals, there are, surprisingly, others who are called apostles, like Andronicus (Romans 16:7); Apollos (1 Corinthians 4:1-13); Barnabas (Acts 14:1-14); and even Jesus (Hebrews 3:1). Even more, Paul, by his own testimony declared, "and last of all He appeared to me also, as to one abnormally born. For I am the least of the apostles and do not even deserve to be called an apostle, because I persecuted the church of God. But by the grace of God I am with I am" (1 Corinthians 15:8-10; Acts 9:15-16; 22:14-15; 26:16-18; and Galatians 1:1). Time and space do not permit further exploration of Paul. These apprentices of Jesus changed the world. Allow me to unfold one profile for our instruction and encouragement to be open and dangerous witnesses. What could be more important?

Peter is our starting place. Since he gets so much attention in the Gospels and Acts, we will also give him greater visibility here. Jesus nicknamed him the "Rock" (*Petros*). His real name was Simon. He is always mentioned first among the apostles. He appears on the pages of Scripture as dominant, opinionated, strong-willed, well-intentioned, prone to speaking before thinking, big-hearted, loud, enthusiastic, flawed, extroverted, and a natural leader. The Gospel writers, especially Mark, pull no punches in painting this particular apostle with warts and all. Some Bible students believe that Mark consulted with Peter in the writing of his Gospel. If that is true, it is no wonder that Mark's portrait of Peter is an honest account of this apostle's many blunders and on-going growth as a disciple of Jesus. He is the disciple who first identifies Jesus as the Promised Messiah (Mark 8:29), the first one to get out of the boat (Matthew 14:29), the first one to speak up at the Transfiguration (Mark 9:5), the first one to declare his faithful allegiance to Jesus, "Even if all fall away, I will not" (Mark 14:29), the first and only disciple willing to draw a sword in defense of Jesus (John 18:10), and the first one to run inside the empty tomb (John 20:6). But, this same Peter is also the one who attempted to rebuke Jesus about predicting His death (Mark 8:32), the one who fearfully sank in the stormy waves of the Sea of Galilee (Matthew 14:30), the one who initially refused to have Jesus wash his feet (John 13:8), the one who did draw that sword mentioned above, the one who bitterly wept over his own betrayal of Jesus (Mark 14:72), and the one who required a three-part challenge and restoration (John 21:15-19). Later on, he will even require a stern, face to face rebuke from Paul for his duplicity regarding the Gentile mission (Galatians 2:11-14). To Peter's credit, he never defended himself. I love this guy.

What you may not know about this man is the way his life ends. Church tradition tells us Peter died in Rome. We don't know how long he had lived in the political center of the Roman Empire, but there is non-biblical support for his presence in that great city. I can't help but think of the words Jesus spoke to Peter, post-resurrection, at the early morning breakfast along the Galilean shoreline: "When you are old you will stretch out your hands, and someone else will dress you and lead you where you do not want to go" (John 21:18). Thirty plus years later, Peter arrived in Rome during a period of intense persecution from Nero. Legend tells us that he saw other Jesus-followers being killed and decided to flee the city. Outside Rome, he encountered a stranger heading into the city, carrying a cross. Peter asked him, "Where are you going?" The man said, "To Rome, to be crucified again." Peter understood, returned to the city, and was martyred for Christ. Tradition says that this apostle was crucified upside down, as a means of proclaiming his unworthiness. I'm drawn to the fact that the "Rock" was still being chiseled and formed for the duration of his life. All of us who witness to Christ are a work in progress. Peter boldly portrays for us "Open Lives: The First and Best Witness is the Life You Live." This apostle is foundational proof that Jesus is faithful in finishing what He started. If you would like to know what happened to the rest of the apostles, go to the back of this book and read the rest of their stories.

WEEK 1: WEDNESDAY;
A CROSS-CULTURAL PERSPECTIVE

THE STORY OF MAHIPAU

Like most children in India, Mahipau was born into a Hindu family and raised as a devout Hindu. At a young age, his passion boiled over into fanaticism as he joined a local extremist group. Their goal: to eradicate Christianity and to promote "Hindutva," a vision for one common nation and race united under Hinduism. Mahipau not only approved of persecuting the local church, but he led by example. He would often verbally attack Christians for their faith and incite riots to beat them. He recounts telling numerous people they could "take the name of any other god... but not Jesus." Hinduism, a religion with over 300 million gods had somehow become exclusive in his mind: "You can worship any god you desire, except for Jesus."

Our culture isn't much different. Our culture applauds the worship and pursuit of money, careers, popularity, prestige, sex, education, knowledge, and even tolerance... but not Jesus. We can take the name of any other god, but not him. That's the one unacceptable pursuit.

Mahipau was a modern-day Saul, driven by self-righteous zeal, legalism, and power. He testifies, "when I was persecuting Christians I had this belief that it was my duty to stop them." Little did he know, his life, like Saul, was about to be changed forever. In a short amount of time, Mahipau's son died, and his wife became terminally ill. As they tried desperately to save her, nothing worked, and she was given one week to live. One day, tormented by hopelessness, Mahipau was confronted by a man. When asked why he was so sad, Mahipau explained his son's recent death and his wife's current sickness. Sorrow, pain, and frustration consumed him.

The man urged him to call on the name of Jesus for healing. Mahipau's response: "shut your mouth and get out of here, I don't need your Jesus." Later that week, in a moment of sheer desperation, Mahipau did the unthinkable. Every morning, he began to call on the name of Jesus: "**Jesus, if you're really a <u>living</u> God, heal my wife.**" "If you're really a living God".... could it be that deep down, in a place he didn't want to admit, he knew that the gods of his youth rang hollow in his time of need? In his most intimate, human moment, these gods were distant, silent, in a word, dead. But somehow, in this moment of desperation, he reaches for a God that is living—Jesus, if you really are a LIVING God, heal my wife.

Three weeks later, Mahipau's wife regained her strength and began a complete recovery. Her miraculous healing led the couple to the one true living God. He had brought them back from the edge of the grave, physically and spiritually. Mahipau and his wife accepted

Christ as Lord and Savior and, consequently, lost everything else. Their entire family disowned them. As a visible leader in the Hindu extremist group, he became a target. His conversion could not go unpunished. He recounts, "we lived in the jungle for 10 months, but I continued to preach and teach them." Mahipau was sharing the gospel with the very people trying to kill him. After two years, he baptized his entire family into Christ.

God was doing the miraculous in and through Mahipau. What's impossible with man is possible with God. As he reflects on the past decade, it's with a willingness of sacrifice we can't possibly fathom: "Almost every month for the last ten years, I've been attacked and beaten by Hindu extremists." (For those counting, that's 100 - 120 attacks). The riots he used to organize are now the same ones planned against him. He's been thrown in jail sixteen times because of his faith. Like the apostle Paul, Mahipau "bears the marks of Christ on his body" (Galatians 6:17). Try to imagine what it would be like, everyday, to kiss your family goodbye, not knowing if you'll see them again this side of eternity.

As he reflects on his story of triumph and persecution, he offers this sobering thought: "The more we're persecuted, the more we pray for strength and endurance so that we will be able to reach more people for Jesus." **The prayer of a "dangerous witness" is not a**

reprieve from the assignment, but the strength and boldness to complete it. Ajai Lall, founder of CICM reminds us that, "as Christians, we see things differently; we see things in the context of eternity." A dangerous witness understands that his or her life is the best witness, and "our light and momentary troubles are achieving for us an eternal glory that far outweighs them all" (2 Cor. 4:17).

If this story were the entirety of Maihpau's testimony, it would be inspiring. It would challenge us to consider the cost of following Christ. It would compel us to take greater risks in living out a Dangerous Witness. It would convict us to throw aside trivial fears of rejection and inadequacy, our desire to fit in, the pressure not to "rock the boat" and boldly step out with the authority and power God promises us (verse). But, as they often say, that's not the end of the story.

Over the past ten years, Mahipau has fearlessly proclaimed the good news of Jesus Christ in word and deed. Despite constant intimidation, beatings, death threats, and jail time, he displays a boldness that the world cannot understand. In the last decade, he baptized over 1,675 people, twenty-two of which have become pastors of their own churches. To put this number in perspective, if every person he baptized gave a five-minute testimony of how Christ has changed their lives, it would take 140 hours, or close to six days, to hear them all.

Mahipau has planted over a dozen churches and believes his best years of service remain ahead of him.

Mahipau reminds us that our first and best witness is the life we live. We only have one chance to give our very best for the King. It is worth it. Are you willing? This is what an "open life" and a dangerous witness look like.

WEEK 1: THURSDAY;
A LOCAL PERSPECTIVE

OPEN LIVES: MEET ROSIE ARCHER

When anyone first meets Rosie Archer, they are typically struck by her straight-forward manner. A conversation with this woman is like encountering someone shaped by pain and the love of Jesus. Rosie is a unique combination of Mother Teresa, Whoopi Goldberg's character in *Sister Act,* and the Bible's Queen of Sheba. She is down to earth, yet classy, toughened, but still tender, wise, but hungry to know more. She is marked by joy, yet seasoned by life. I first met her at Lincoln Christian University's Hargrove School while guest lecturing in one of her courses.

Rosie lives out this week's theme in a very intentional and Spirit-led way. She has experienced life in a manner that few of us ever do. Her grandmother was brutally murdered when Rosie was about nine years old. With heartache and deep confusion, she asked her mother, "Where did grandma go?" Her mother replied, "To heaven." Rosie can still easily tear up when she recalls those memories. This strong woman grew up looking out of the window of that Chicago West Side apartment and saying to herself, "I wish I were a different person."

Life is hard in Chicago's inter-city. Rosie, the oldest of ten siblings, has known hunger and deprivation. Richard C. Crane Technical Preparatory High School on West Jackson Boulevard, from which Rosie graduated, is not known for producing millionaires or people of power and influence. Seventy-four percent of the students are from low income families. Twenty percent are special education students. The texture of Rosie's story is incomplete without one more sobering fact. Rosie's father was shot on those same streets, and the injuries left him paralyzed. How did she come to realize that the first and best witness to Jesus is the life she lives? Our conversation for this chapter went something like this.

How long have you been a believer?

"It was November 8th, 2006, and I was reading Rick Warren's *Purpose-Driven Life.* I was taking notes, writing in my journal, and I realized how empty I felt inside. I decided that day to make a contract with God. I had, up to that point, spent my whole life running from Him. I had experimented with so many other avenues in trying to find meaning and purpose. It was like I was saying to God, 'I'll give you a try.' During my reading of that book, a woman witnessed to me, and I really met Jesus for the first time. Several months earlier, outside Wal-Mart, I asked a friend of mine why a certain lady was so nice to her. 'She's a Christian,' my friend replied. I asked, 'What's a Christian?' I had no idea what it meant to be in a relationship with Jesus. In July, I attended church and saw so many happy people, and I wondered to myself why I was so sad. One of my children was struggling in grade school, and I recall walking home in tears, feeling like it was my fault. I thought that, somehow, I had failed as a mother. God began to reveal more and more of Himself to me. During this season of my life, I had taken a trip back to Iowa City, Iowa, where I had previously spent three years working and making poor decisions. The police had even told me, 'You have to leave Iowa City.' So, I prayed to God, 'If you get me out of Iowa City, I will be different.' But no one can become a new person on their own. Only God can do that. When I returned from that trip to Iowa City, I was seeking to be someone different, and that's when I read *Purpose-Driven Life*. I was immersed December 3, 2006."

How did you end up at ECC?

"Believe it or not, God came to me in a dream. He directed me to leave a particular church I was attending. I shared this dream with a close friend of mine, and she said I should pray to see if it was something that the Lord really wanted. So I did. I ended up attending a single mom's Bible study, and I began to make connections. I met Nicki Green, Lisa Miller Rich, and others. They genuinely loved me. The first Sunday I came to ECC, I heard Mike Baker pray, and I was awed by that. I had never heard anyone pray so much. Eventually, after that season of personal prayer, I decided to stay at Eastview. Five years later, I'm still here, along with my children, Erica and James, serving in the GEMS (God Embracing Moms who are Single) ministry as a Production Assistant with our worship team and sometimes meeting people at the cross after our worship services."

How does Open Lives: The first and Best Witness is the Life You Live fit you?

"I've worked at the Qik-n-EZ (local gas station) for the past five years. I meet hurting people, angry people, sad people, and a lot of single moms. I interact with them and with my co-workers about Jesus. Initially, the focus was on me. I wanted people to see Rosie, and I wanted to make a pay check. But over time, God began to change me. I hated the job at first, but God was placing small miracles in front of me. People would provide me with financial gifts just when I needed help the most. One lady even gave me two- hundred and fifty dollars in a small envelope. She said that God had put me on her heart. I've had mean-spirited customers say to me, 'Thank you for being kind to me today.' In 2009, God made it clear to me that this was my mission field. I can relate with people who are struggling. I know what it is like to have nothing. God took my past, and He completely put my life back together. He made me a new creation. I want to speak life into people. That's Jesus, not me."

The first and best witness is the life you live.

WEEK 1: FRIDAY;
A PERSONAL PERSPECTIVE

As we near the completion of the first week of "OPEN," let's review how we've been inspired by various perspectives:

- ♦ A Biblical Perspective from 1 Peter 3:15
- ♦ An Historical Perspective of the Apostle Peter
- ♦ A Cross-Cultural Perspective of Mahipau (church planter in India)
- ♦ A Local Perspective in Rosie Archer (member of Eastview Christian Church)

Now, we encourage you to examine and to expand our "personal perspective" as we contemplate and apply these stories and principles in our daily lives. As the subtitle for this chapter suggests, "your first and best witness is the life you live." The consistency and substance of our faith either plays, arrests, or advances our witness. The deeply personal question left to answer is, "Am I a person of integrity who demonstrates consistency between my beliefs, words, and lifestyle?" Consider the following verses that speak to the significance of our integrity:

> "May my heart be blameless toward your decrees, that I may not be put to shame" (Psalm 119:80).

> "He holds victory in store for the upright, he is a shield to those whose walk is blameless, for he guards the course of the just and protects the way of his faithful ones" (Proverbs 2:7-8).

"The man of integrity walks securely, but he who takes crooked paths will be found out" (Proverbs 10:9).

"Now this is our boast: Our conscience testifies that we have conducted ourselves in the world, and especially in our relations with you, in the holiness and sincerity that are from God" (2 Corinthians 1:12).

"In everything set them an example by doing what is good. In your teaching show integrity, seriousness and soundness of speech that cannot be condemned, so that those who oppose you may be ashamed because they have nothing bad to say about us" (Titus 2:7-8).

Admittedly, this pursuit of integrity is life-long. There is grace when we fall short, but this grace is a motivation to pursue integrity all the more (Romans 7:7-8:1). On our better days, we are driven to prayer when we consider the many eyes that watch us live out lives of faith. Paul Lee Tan once shared a moving story of a man's integrity on display:

AFTER HIS SUNDAY MESSAGES, the pastor of a church in London got on the trolley Monday morning to return to his study downtown. He paid his fare, and the trolley driver gave him too much change. The pastor sat down and fumbled the change and looked it over, counted it eight or ten times. And, you know the rationalization, "It's wonderful how God provides." He realized he was tight that week, and this change was just about what he would need to break even, or at least enough for his lunch. He wrestled with himself all the way down that old trolley trail that led to his office. Finally, he came to the stop, and he got up, couldn't live with himself, walked up to the trolley driver, and said, "Here, you gave me too much change.

You made a mistake." The driver said, "No, it was no mistake. You see, I was in your church last night when you spoke on honesty, and I thought I would put you to the test." (Swindoll, 1998, p. 304)

We are not likely to face such manufactured tests of our integrity, but our integrity will be tested nonetheless. We're put to the test as our words and ways are observed by our children. We're consciously and subconsciously examined by our co-workers as our "open lives" display or betray our proclaimed faith. Such realizations create a holy tension within us, causing each of us to long for genuine humility and holiness. We want to remain authentic and consistent while (at the same time) authentically changing to become more Christ-like. This is no simple task! Before running off to the next segment of this book or the demands of the day, choose one of the following activities for personal application:

♦ Examine the life you live. Is there activity that needs to increase? Is there activity that needs to decrease?

♦ Consider the cost of maintaining your integrity. How does this cost compare with compromising your integrity?

♦ Invite your spouse or a member of your small group to help you evaluate the impact of your "witness." Are there any blind spots that can be lovingly addressed? Are there any victories that have been undetected?

♦ Journal about the one or two concepts from this chapter that most inspire you.

As we conclude this chapter, note the sweet surrender found in the following Puritan prayer of Christlikeness. May this prayer be our prayer as we seek to live "open lives":

Father of Jesus … May my words and works allure others to the highest walks of faith and love! May loiterers be quickened to greater diligence by my example! May worldlings be won to delight in acquaintance with thee! May the timid and irresolute be warned of coming doom by my zeal for Jesus! Cause me to be a mirror of thy grace, to show others the joy of thy service, may my lips be well-tuned cymbals sounding thy praise … Help me to walk as Jesus walked, my only Saviour and perfect model, his mind my inward guest, his meekness my covering garb…" (Bennett, 1975, p. 248)

WEEK 1: SATURDAY

On Saturdays, throughout our study of "OPEN," we will pause to memorize one Scripture reference and to contemplate one thought-provoking question.

> "But in your hearts set apart Christ as Lord. Always be prepared to give an answer to everyone who asks you to give the reason for the hope that you have. But do this with gentleness and respect" (1 Peter 3:15).

As you reflect on the past year of your life, think of the times you have been asked to give a "reason for the hope that you have." What does this reason reveal about the "openness" of your life?

WEEK TWO

Open Arms

"Connecting with those apart from Christ"

MONDAY; A BIBLICAL PERSPECTIVE

"I want to eat less often with saints and more often with sinners. I want some of my best friends to be lost - but not for long"
(Chambers, 2009, p.14).

Principle: Find and/or create opportunities to hang out with lost people.

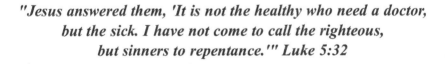

"Jesus answered them, 'It is not the healthy who need a doctor, but the sick. I have not come to call the righteous, but sinners to repentance.'" Luke 5:32

Probably like you, I have attended a lot of parties in my lifetime. Most of them celebrated birthdays, anniversaries, holidays, and graduations. Most of these parties predictably included cake and refreshments, cards and gifts, and conversations that begin with, "I remember when" and "good luck." These parties are enjoyable enough.

After all, how can you mess up laughter, love, and sugar?! But there have been some parties I have enjoyed more than others: gatherings where, instead of the awesome fellowship found in Christian community, there was freshly enjoyable relationships with non-believers and a spiritual purpose.

In Luke chapter five, we find such a party at the home of Levi (more readily recognized as Matthew) where Jesus and a bunch of sinners shared a meal at the same table. It all began with Levi sitting at his usual place of business—the tax collector's booth. Tax collectors were hated by Jews for many reasons. First, they were agents of the Roman government collecting taxes for occupiers and oppressors of the Jewish nation. Second, most tax collectors were dishonest, regularly over-charging the public and keeping the difference for themselves. They were among the wealthiest of the people. Third, tax collectors were judged as gross sinners because they did not observe the ritual and practice of Moses' law. To a first century Jew, "tax collector" was synonymous with "sinner"!

Jesus thought differently. He actually invited Levi, a tax collector, to become one of his students (the Greek word for student is *mathetes* and is usually translated "disciple"). The invitation was simple. "Follow me," Jesus said when Levi looked up, expecting his next disgruntled tax payer. Jesus' gaze was so compelling that Levi could not resist the call of the Savior, and he immediately left every-thing to follow. But Levi didn't just follow; he decided to invite his circle of friends into his new life with Jesus. Yes, his irreligious, spir-itually-outcast, non-God fearing friends were invited to hang out with the most spiritual person the world has ever seen. Levi threw a party inviting both Jesus and his non-spiritual friends.

This may surprise you, coming from a preacher, but my favorite parties are with pagans. I'll tell you why later in this chapter. Just to be clear, I think Christians should party regularly with one another to celebrate the love they have found in Christ and the joy of the church community. I believe in biblical fellowship, and I frequently have awesome social times with dear Christian brothers and sisters. In fact, laughing with, eating with, sharing stories with, praying with, crying with, and rejoicing with those who are fellow Christ follow-ers is one of the great benefits of being a part of God's family. However, as a pastor, if I am not intentional, I will spend time only with Christians and lose contact with the very people I'm supposed to reach—those outside of Christ. I am not alone; statistics show that, "once the average person becomes a believer in Christ, he or she loses contact with all unbelieving friends within two years" (Patton, 2004, n.p). If you are a Christian, does this statistic describe you?

Several years ago, my youngest son was playing his final recreational league basketball game as a fifth grader. He had played ball with several of the same kids for many years, but since they would all attend different middle schools in the coming year, most of them would likely not play together again. Over the years, my wife and I had watched countless games with the parents of these boys and had developed a casual acquaintance with them. But as the final minutes ticked off the clock of the final game, something unexpected and exciting happened. One of the moms invited all the parents to an end-of-the-year party at her house. I saw this invitation as a God opportunity, so my wife and I readily accepted the invitation. Soon, we found ourselves heading to a strange home to hang out with a bunch of non-Christian people we barely knew with a prayer that we would represent Jesus well. As it turns out, we had a blast too!

Jesus also accepted Matthew's invitation to the party, which brought criticism from the spiritually elite of his day. The religious leaders thought that a godly man should stay away from sinful people, but Jesus thought differently. His mission was not to hang out with spiritual people, but to spend time influencing the lives of those farthest from God. If He were here today, He would rather hang out with prostitutes on the street than speak at your church on Sunday. Why would Jesus rather open His arms to sinners than hang out with saints? And what can we learn from this story in Luke 5:27-32?

We know why Jesus accepted this party invitation from Levi. Jesus' actions were judged and questioned by the religious leaders, and his answer gives us insight into the heart of the savior. He went to this party because He cared for these people. He was dedicated to calling the unrighteous and healing the sick. In fact, the reasons given in this story for Jesus' presence at a pagan party are the same for me preferring pagan parties and the same reasons I'm encouraging you to find or to create similar opportunities. Here are three reasons to party with the lost.

There are people in our lives who are easy for us to reach

Levi was a tax collector, which meant that he could easily relate to other tax collectors. He didn't throw a party for fishermen or black-smiths or winemakers. He intentionally spent time with those he could relate to and those who could relate to him. The major "duh" moment in sharing your faith comes when you realize that God has given each of us a circle of co-workers, fellow students, social friends, neighbors, and family members to whom we naturally relate. These are the people who are most likely to respond to our witness about Christ because we are already a part of their worlds. Tax collectors can most comfortably share Jesus with other tax collectors. For us, this example reflects how each of us has a group of people with whom we can most naturally cultivate relationships and share our faith. Nursing students have an "in" with other nursing students; teammates can influence teammates; assembly line workers best reach other assembly line workers; executives speak the language of other executives, and stay-at-home moms relate best to other stay-at-home moms. I believe there are lost people in each of our lives that only we can reach. Have you ever thought that maybe God, in His providence, has placed certain people in your life so that you can share Jesus with them?

We are not set against sinners, so we can be comfortable in relationships with them

Unlike the Pharisees, who stood in opposition to sinful people and therefore avoided them, Jesus was very comfortable with lost people. In the Luke story, we find that Jesus is accused of "eating and drinking with tax collectors and sinners." This description gives us some insight into Jesus' ability to relate to all people. He was comfortable reclining at the table, having casual conversation, asking questions that showed He cared, listening to others, and sharing food with strangers. The common meal is one of the most human experiences, and Jesus shows His compassion and love by simply being around the table. He can talk with these friends of Levi because He genuinely cares about them.

You and I can enter into social relationships with anyone because we all share common human realities. Every human faces disappointments. Every human has family and relationships. Every human has a journey and a story. Every human has a dream for the future. Every human has a passion, talent, or gift. Every human gets hungry, thirsty, and tired. What's the point? Though they may not have Jesus as savior, every person we encounter has more in common with us than they have differences. This commonality means we can find comfortable conversation and relationship with anyone if we simply love them as fellow humans.

Believe you have a remedy that everyone needs

The final reason Jesus gives for hanging out with sinners is that they need what He has. He sees beyond the physical reality and the social position of these tax collector's lives to the deep spiritual illness they have called "sin." Jesus knows that, though these men have possessions, power, and position, they are lost in their sin. He spends time with them in a social setting because He knows they need life that only He can give. Christ followers are people who have found Jesus to be the answer for every need in their lives. As savior, He has taken our sins away, and, as Lord, He guides us where we need to go. We enter into relationships with non-believers because we believe that they need what we have. No matter how content and happy those around us may seem, if they do not have Jesus in their lives, then they have an unseen terminal illness brought on by the sin that contaminates this world. Like our Leader, we hang out with lost people because we know how much better life is with the remedy of grace and forgiveness that only Christ can offer.

The party with our basketball friends was a blast. Thankfully, these friends were not ashamed to offer wine, beer, and stronger drinks along with Coke, coffee, and lemonade because a pastor was coming. They didn't shy away from "colorful" speech. As a Christian, I chose not to make any weird "Jesus-guilt-trip comments," and everyone else chose simply to be themselves. The conversation centered on our kids, our jobs, our life journeys, and, yes, our spiritual backgrounds. Honestly, I didn't force a thing, but mid-way through the night, we were talking about church, religion, and Jesus. The amazing part is that the conversation wasn't that hard. All I did was put myself in a place where I could hang out with sinners, and the Holy Spirit did the rest. So now I'm constantly looking for opportunities to hang out with lost people so that, in relationship, I can naturally introduce them to the Friend they really need. I hope you will do the same.

WEEK 2: TUESDAY;
AN HISTORICAL PERSPECTIVE

POLYCARP
AN HISTORICAL PERSPECTIVE

The name "Polycarp" sounds foreign to a lot of us. It might even conjure up a picture of denture adhesive, but Polycarp is not inter-changeable with PoliGrip. Important figures in the early centuries of the church like Irenaeus, theologian and church father (130-202 AD), Tertullian, North African church father (160-225), and Jerome, priest, theologian, and translator of the Bible into Latin (347-420 AD), all tell us that Polycarp was a faithful witness to Jesus Christ. You might remember that the original meaning behind the word "martyr" is "witness." Words, of course, sometimes change their meanings. "Martyr," today, typically describes someone who choos-es to suffer persecution or death rather than to deny Jesus. Experts tell us there are more Christian martyrs today than there were in the first century of the early church. Polycarp was a martyr for Jesus somewhere around 155 AD, though some suggest a later date of 168 AD. Here is what we know of this remarkable witness's life.

Few exemplify in church history the theme we are trying to address this week – "Open Arms: Connecting with Those Apart from Christ"—like Polycarp. His long life, 69 to 155 AD, is not well known. We do know that he was a vibrant Christian witness to those in and around Smyrna, Asia, modern day Izmar, Turkey. He was a passionate defender of Christianity and orthodoxy. Irenaeus, who was raised in Smyrna, tells us that he heard Polycarp teach and preach. That same Irenaeus tells us that Polycarp had come under the influence of several of the early apostles and was specifically discipled by the Apostle John. That fact makes this witness the last living link to Jesus' own disciples! The remarkable story of Polycarp's death is prefaced by a trip to Rome in order to see his friend and fellow bishop, Anicetus. Again, it is Irenaeus who records for us that famous visit where Polycarp and Anicetus discussed questions about Christian practice and the Easter date. Upon Polycarp's return to Smyrna, he was arrested by city officials.

A pagan festival was underway in the Smyrna arena, and Polycarp was brought before the Roman governor. Perhaps, as a Bible reader, you might be recalling Jesus' words in Revelation to the church at Smyrna: "Do not be afraid of what you are about to suffer...Be faithful, even to the point of death, and I will give you the crown of life" (Revelation 2:10). Polycarp was told, "Swear by the fortune of Caesar. Take the oath, and I will release you. Curse Christ!" Polycarp's now-famous reply was, "Eighty-six years have I served the Lord Jesus Christ, and He never once wronged me. How can I blaspheme my King who has saved me?" According to Irenaeus, the governor responded, "I have wild beasts ready, and I will throw you to them if you do not change your mind." Polycarp boldly declared, "Let them come, for my purpose is unchangeable." Tradition tells us that the angry Roman proconsul retorted, "If the wild beasts don't scare you, then I will burn you with fire." This apprentice to Jesus was unmoved by the threats: "You threaten me with a fire which will burn for an hour and then will go out, but you are ignorant of the fire of the future judgment of God reserved for the everlasting torment of the ungodly. But why do you delay? Bring on the beasts, or the fire, or whatever you choose; you shall not move me? to deny Christ, my Lord and Savior." Then the governor instructed the local herald or town crier to shout three times for everyone to hear: "Polycarp has professed himself a Christian!" The hate-filled crowd screamed and chanted that Polycarp be killed. A large bonfire was created. Initially, the plan was to nail Polycarp to the center stake, but he told his accusers that it was unnecessary to do so: "Leave me as I am; He who gives me strength to endure the fire will enable me to remain still within the fire." So, Polycarp was simply tied to the stake. His last prayer was simple: "O Father, I thank You, that You have called me to this day and hour and have counted me worthy to receive my place among the number of the holy martyrs. Amen." The enormous fire was lit. The flames engulfed his body, but the strangest wonder unfolded. The flames did not burn his body. Eyewitnesses recalled, "He was in the midst of the fire, not as burning flesh but as gold and silver refined in the furnace. And we smelled such a sweet aroma of incense or some other precious spice." When the governor realized his prisoner was not suffering, the executioner was ordered to stab Polycarp with the sword. Polycarp's last moments were marked by another miracle. Once the executioner drove the sword into Polycarp's side, so much blood flowed from the cut that it put out the fire! This lover of Christ practiced a long obedience and was unashamed to invite all that he met into a living and vibrant relationship with Jesus.

WEEK 2: WEDNESDAY;
A CROSS-CULTURAL PERSPECTIVE

THE STORY OF SANJAY

In a moment of honest, unfiltered, soul searching transparency, ask yourself the following three questions:

♦ "What am I willing to do to connect with people who don't know Jesus?"

♦ "How much am I really willing to sacrifice?"

♦ "What's the unspoken limit in my mind and heart as to what I'll sacrifice to share the ridiculous love of Jesus with people who are eternally lost?

Though we may feel tempted to speed through them, the questions above are anything but hypothetical. We answer them every day by the choices we make. That's what makes it so humbling to meet a man like Sanjay. His story will break you. It makes you uncomfortable. It challenges you to re-evaluate what Jesus meant when he said, "follow me." Just like you, Sanjay had to wrestle with these questions, but he quickly resolved to give his entire life to God, no matter the cost.

As a young man growing up in India, Sanjay accepted Christ as Lord and Savior and was quickly fueled to share this good news with the lost of Central India. He enrolled at one of the biblical training academies at Central India Christian Mission (CICM). Over the next year, Sanjay would be trained in theology, preaching, and church planting and would take a crash course in losing his life to save it (Matthew 16:25).

Upon Sanjay's graduation, despite the dangers awaiting them, Sanjay and his wife, Gulshan, headed out into the unknown. They went to a completely unreached area in Central India, home to no known Christians. The area was controlled by Hindu extremists that forbid Christians to live in the region. But God was gracious and, despite constant threats and intimidation, Sanjay and Gulshan faithfully shared the good news of Jesus with the local villages. Toward the end of their first year, the local church they planted was averaging three-hundred people in attendance. Gulshan led a children's Sunday school program that averaged 150 children each week. As people were baptized and the church grew, theChristians were threatened and harassed. They had quickly become targets. Through it all, they clung to the promises of Christ and the love they had for each other. Sanjay and Gulshan took Jesus at his word in Luke 12:4 when he said, "I tell you, my friends, do not be afraid of those who kill the body and after that can do no more."

As time marched on, one Sunday after worship, Sanjay needed to take Gulshan to the hospital for a health problem. The trip would take over an hour. On their motorbike, they faithfully weaved their way towards the city and passed through an area of dense jungle. They didn't realize they were being followed until they entered the jungle covering. It was too late when they realized a trap had been set. Three motorcycles, carrying a group of extremists, stopped their motorbike and forced them off the path. With the cover of the jungle protecting them from onlookers, the men pulled out iron rods and began to attack Sanjay and Gulshan. The two victims were completely defenseless. As Sanjay desperately tried to protect his bride, the men struck his arms with such force that they shattered his arms. The next blow brought the sickening sound of the iron crushing Sanjay's forehead. In an instant, he was knocked unconscious, slumping over on the jungle path.

Two days later, Sanjay slowly opened his eyes to find himself in an ICU room. He'd been badly beaten, had almost died, and had been unconscious for the last two days. As soon as he was able to speak, he asked for his wife, Gulshan. In a moment that none of us can understand this side of eternity, Sanjay was told that his wife had passed away. After he was knocked unconscious, the men stood over his wife and beat her to death. Due to the circumstances of her death and the condition of her body, her funeral had been held the day before, while Sanjay was still unconscious. He never got to say goodbye.

Words fail in moments like these as we cling to the promise of Romans 8:26 that the Spirit helps us in our weakness. When we don't have the strength to pray, the Spirit will intercede for us through groans. He did this through Sanjay's tears. Slowly, Sanjay began to recover physically but was emotionally devastated. He returned to the place where his calling began. He went back to the CICM Bible academy to grieve, to receive counseling, and to begin the slow process of healing. After two months, Sanjay made the incredible decision that he was to return to the people who threatened and harassed him. He was to go back to the people who rejected him. He was to minister to the people who had attacked him and murdered his wife. It was with these people that Sanjay wanted to re-connect and to share the love of Christ. Over time, Sanjay would do just that. He would travel back, this time alone, as a physical representation of Jesus' unconditional love. This decision would appear as motivated by pure insanity, except to a God who gave his life for people while they were still enemies. Over time, God was faithful, and Sanjay's living testimony changed lives. The church doubled in size and continues to grow. Many have entered the kingdom of God because of this wounded healer. But Sanjay's story isn't over; in fact, there is much to be written. He continues to live out this life of connecting with the lost. Every day, he's reminded by visible and emotional scars that God is using him to change eternity.

Sanjay's testimony turns us back toward the questions posed at the beginning of this chapter. What are you willing to do to connect with the lost, and how much are you willing to sacrifice? What is your unspoken limit that, maybe, you've never shared with another human soul, what you're really willing to sacrifice? Your story will be different than Sanjay's and Gulshan's. God never writes the same story twice. Unfortunately, you and I will never meet Gulshan on this side of eternity. Most of us will never meet Sanjay. But you can be assured of this: one day we'll meet. And with tears in our eyes, they'll introduce us to the hundreds, if not thousands, of redeemed saints who were lost but have now been brought into the kingdom through their faithful lives. What a holy moment. My prayer is that you and I will have people to introduce them to as well. How are you abandoning a life of safety and security to connect with the lost around you?

WEEK 2: THURSDAY;

OPEN ARMS: MEET MARK HAPKE

My first impression of Mark Hapke is that he is marked by a gentle soul. There is a kindness that quickly surfaces in him, mirroring the living presence of Jesus. His tenderness of heart for the Lord and for people is quickly evident. This week's interview is all about connecting with those people we meet who don't know Christ. I bluntly asked Mark while visiting with him at the Mitsubishi plant where he works, "What are you praying for?" Without hesitation, he responded, "Opportunity. I pray every day, 'not my will, but Your will be done.'" Allow me to introduce you to Mark and, in turn, his passion for introducing people to Jesus.

Mark was born in Peoria and raised in Pekin. His Central Illinois roots are strong. He has been married to his wife, Paula, for thirty-three years, and they are the parents of six children, ranging in ages from eight to thirty-one. Their youngest daughter, Lia, was adopted from China. Talk about open arms! It doesn't take long to discern how much Mark loves his wife and family. He started working at Mitsubishi twenty-five years ago and has experienced multiple job shifts and promotions. Normally, when we think of factory work, we conjure pictures of places and sometimes even people who are hardened, irreligious, and indifferent to the Gospel. But Mark sees things differently. He considers himself an ambassador for Christ at the plant. He was gracious enough to give me a tour of the facility before we sat down to talk through his spiritual journey. I noticed on several occasions how much he lived out Colossians 3:23 as he described for me the intricacies of car manufacturing: "Whatever you do, work at it with all your heart, as working for the Lord, not for men."

Where did your spiritual journey begin?

"I was raised as a Missouri Synod Lutheran. My biblical grounding was solid, and I deeply appreciated my spiritual roots, but I somehow managed to miss Jesus."

How did that happen? How did you miss Jesus?

"I had gone to church my whole life, but, ironically, I continued to manage to not give Christ my whole life. I kept parts of it for me— what I watched on TV, what I listened to, my language, what I gave back to the Lord, and all sorts of other areas that were not yet surrendered. In 1991-1992, we began to attend ECC's Saturday evening service. Week after week, the messages seemed to be just for me, as I saw areas of my life that needed to be given over. Paula was raised Catholic, and she was experiencing the same things I was. Our journey has been in a series of segments, rather than a Paul-like-

Damascus-Road experience (Acts 9). We shifted toward Jesus in degrees."

Was there a defining moment in that shifting?

"Yes, we came to a point where we needed to make a decision, not only for us, but for our family. Only God can work these things out perfectly. We met with Bob Knapp and talked about a decision to be baptized. By this time, Jesus had stepped out of the history book, and I had begun a personal relationship with Him. Both Paula and I had been baptized as infants, but Bob baptized us in the believers' baptism. We eventually landed in a small group, and that also proved to be a significant mile-marker in our Christian walk."

Where does your burden for people get birthed?

"ECC emphasized the sharing of the Gospel. In those days, we had an annual event called 'Easter at the Arena' where we gathered as one large body of believers at Redbird Arena on ISU's campus. The impact on the community was significant. It gave people like me an opportunity to talk about Jesus and invite others to our Easter services. I don't see myself as an extrovert, but I felt compelled to move out of my comfort zone. One man, who was at first very resistant to the Gospel, accepted an invitation and brought his family one Easter. Today, he is an elder in his church, and all his family are Christ-followers."?

How does this passion get expressed in the work place?

"I brought some sermon tapes to work. People often saw them on my desk and would ask about one in particular, *From Here to Eternity*. It gave me the bridge to speak of my relationship with Jesus. Several vendors began borrowing tape-packs to listen to while driving. I had assumed that one man, in particular, was already a Christian. I came to learn later that, through those messages, he gave his life to Christ behind the steering wheel of his car. When he was transferred to China for five years, they became his lifeline, and I just received two tape-packs back from him with a thank you note. Other tapes, with other vendors, have travelled throughout the Midwest and to the east coast. I have no idea who all listened to them. Only God could orchestrate that! I'm constantly watching for open opportunities for talking with people about Christ. I pray a prayer regularly: 'Lord, open the door, open my mouth, and open their heart.' It's a prayer God loves to answer. I believe in Divine appointments. Some people plant the seed of the Gospel, some water, some cultivate, and some get to harvest. I'm simply along for the ride. God is the evangelist, and I get to partner with Him. The role God chooses for me may be small and brief, yet vitally important."

Mark Hapke is building more than cars ready for the road; he is building lives ready for eternity.

WEEK 2: FRIDAY;
A PERSONAL PERSPECTIVE

This week we've been challenged to demonstrate "open arms" by connecting with those apart from Christ. In our second week of this study, we've already introduced:

- ♦ A Biblical Perspective from Luke 5:27-32 (Jesus with Levi)
- ♦ An Historical Perspective of Polycarp (disciple of the Apostle John)
- ♦ A Cross-Cultural Perspective of Sanjay (church planter in India)
- ♦ A Local Perspective in Mark Hapke (member of Eastview Christian Church)

I think you'll agree that we've compiled inspirational examples from both near and far, recent and historical, simply shocking and shockingly simple. Now, we are challenged to consider our own response for the call to "open arms." How do you and I personally connect with those apart from Christ?

In his book *Radical Outreach*, George G. Hunter III unfolds five piercing questions for congregations that need to move "from tradition to mission" in their pursuit of people who do not know Jesus as Lord and Savior. His questions are derived from John 4:1-42 where Jesus encounters the woman at the well. While the questions were intended for church leaders, it may be beneficial for each of us to reflect on these questions about our level of interaction with non-Christians.

♦ **Do we want to know them?** Are we sincerely interested in those who have yet to entrust their lives to Christ?

♦ **Are we willing to go where they are?** Do we actively meet people on their turf, or do we passively wait for people to come to us?

♦ **Are we willing to spend time with them?** Do we love people enough to invest time into relationships with them?

♦ **Do we want secular and outside-the-establishment people in our churches?** Let's be honest … outreach can be messy. People who have yet to become familiar with "church etiquette" may be perceived as threatening to some. Does our love for the lost outweigh the discomfort of our differences?

♦ **Are we willing for our church to become their church too?** This question does not suggest compromise on our mission or message. Instead, it compels us to assess any unnecessary barriers that are intentionally or unintentionally constructed in our patterns and practices. In short, "church is not so much a refuge *from* the world as a rescue shop and redemption center *in* it and *for* it" (Sweet, 1999, p. 78).

I'd like to suggest that the "us" and "them" language is not "us vs. them," but "us for them." The use of these pronouns is not meant to be divisive, but distinctive. As we will discuss in the coming weeks, we have a message and ministry of reconciliation (2 Corinthians 5:19-21). By God's grace, we believe that Eastview Christian Church is characterized by a hearty "yes" response to each of these questions. Now, how about you?

Last week, we discussed the notion that, "your first and best witness is the life you live." Our lives are not lived in solitary confinement, but in the ebb and flow of our society. Our personal integrity (moral authority) matters. But this next piece of the puzzle is also critical. With whom are you rubbing shoulders? What natural and intentional opportunities are available for your relationships with non-Christians? As we sift through a variety of great examples in this chapter, commit to at least one of the following in your personal application:

♦ Pray for the Holy Spirit to increase your awareness of one or two people in your sphere of influence who do not know Jesus. Begin to pray for them daily, looking for opportunities to "open your arms" to them.

♦ Which of the five questions from this reading cause you the most strain? What action will you take to reconcile your answer to be most Christ-like?

♦ Discuss this week's reading with your small group, seeking the group's insights and prayer support.

♦ Recall a time when someone displayed "open arms" for you in the past. Send this person an encouraging email this week, thanking them for reaching out to you.

♦ In 1 Corinthians 9:22-23, the Apostle Paul writes, "To the weak I became weak, to win the weak. I have become all things to all men so that by all possible means I might save some. I do all this for the sake of the gospel, that I may share in its blessings." Meditate on this passage and how you might apply it in your life this week.

WEEK 2: SATURDAY

On Saturdays throughout our study of "OPEN," we will pause to memorize one Scripture reference and to contemplate one thought-provoking question.

> "We loved you so much that we were delighted to share with you not only the gospel of God but our lives as well, because you had become so dear to us" (1 Thessalonians 2:8).

In our culture, it is widely understood that time is our greatest commodity. In what ways have you invested precious time into the life of someone outside of our faith circle? In other words, how are you intentionally sharing your life with someone who doesn't know the Author of Life?

WEEK THREE

OPEN WITNESS
"WHAT IS YOUR STORY?"

MONDAY; A BIBLICAL PERSPECTIVE

"When you tell your story, the critical contrast to draw for some-
one is this: What difference has Christ really made in your life?
In other words, what were you like before Christ, and now what
are you like after you've asked Christ to intervene?"
(Hybels, 2006, p.122).

❖

Principle: Everyone has a story.

❖

"I tell you the truth, whoever hears my word and believes in him
who sent me has eternal life and will not be condemned;
he has crossed over from death to life." John 5:24

Several years ago, Eastview offered an invitation to "cross over" from the death of this world to the life that can be found only in Jesus Christ. The invitation doesn't sound that exciting, I know. Most churches offer invitations to follow Jesus. But this invitation was different because it came at the end of a sermon series that called our people to demonstrate their inward reality of faith physically. What happened on that Sunday morning became, for me and for our church, a powerful spiritual visual that depicted the differences in our lives before and after Christ.

One week before this commitment Sunday, a builder from our church began the construction of a bridge at the front of our auditorium to represent our preaching theme over a series of Sundays. Each week, we preached the sermons from the middle of this bridge. Now, if you are visualizing an ordinary run-of-the-mill foot bridge, I need to give you a better picture. It was a real bridge. At fifteen feet wide, it spanned sixty feet from one side to the other. I was assured that, if we wanted to, we could drive a car across it with no problem!

The week of invitation came, and at the end of the sermon we had a time of musical worship set aside for the congregation to respond. Three basic responses were offered: cross the bridge of faith for the first time to accept Jesus as Lord and Savior. Cross the bridge as a sign of recommitment to leaving sin behind. Cross the bridge as a reminder of your story of life change from death to life. Nearly every person in attendance walked the bridge, each representing an individual story of faith.

If you know me, you know tears come easy for me, so it's no surprise that I was crying in public...again. What moved me most was the great diversity displayed on the bridge that day. Every shape, size, color and social class was represented. Couples crossed holding hands. Elderly limped across with canes. Many crossed in wheel chairs while others walked confidently with head held high. Some moved slowly and deliberately, nearly stopping as they crossed the midway point. Many shed tears as the simple crossing reminded them of their journeys. I was overwhelmed with the representation of hundreds of journeys. It's true, everyone has a story, and, in these moments, the walk across the bridge represented each of them.

A necessary part of Christ-following is being willing to tell the story of your life openly. An open witness is simply knowing and telling others about the difference Jesus has made in our lives. The English Bible sometimes translates "witness" as "testimony." Your witness is simply telling the facts of your life as you understand them. There is no "right" or "wrong" story of your life, and every one is a unique encounter with God through His Son Jesus. Don't worry; you don't have to be a speech maker. There is no need for a lengthy speech that gives every detail of the journey. There are just a few facts to include when you are sharing your faith. According to John 5:24, there are three essential elements that all Christians should include in their stories.

When did you hear who Jesus was?

No story of faith can begin without first hearing the saving word of Jesus, his purpose, his mission, and his promise. Jesus originally said, "whoever hears these words of mine..." to a living audience of Galilean peasants who were looking for a promised king, but his words have continued to echo for two-thousand years. We still hear Jesus' word through the teaching of our parents, the preaching of the church, and the witness of our friends. When did you first understand that Jesus had come to save you and to be The Lord of your life?

Some first heard of Jesus as a little child, raised in Christian homes and in the church. Some first discovered His love at the lowest point of their lives as they searched for meaning. Some stumbled unexpectedly into a relationship with Christ through the words of a friend. Some heard a sermon at the right time. Some were searching for truth in an academic setting and found Jesus to be the answer. Everyone who has ever been a Christ follower should be able to articulate when they first heard of Jesus.

When did you make a conscious decision of faith?

Hearing about Jesus' love is not enough. You can do nothing to earn His love, and you can do nothing to remove His love, but for His grace to become a part of your life, you must embrace it. This embrace is called faith or believing in Jesus. Jesus says, we must hear and "believe in him who sent me." There is no salvation apart from faith in God and his son Jesus, who He sent. But what does believing in God through Jesus mean?

The Greek word in John 5:24 that is translated "believe" is the word *pisteuo*. Its root, *pistis*, is translated "faith" and both words indicate a deep conviction of and confidence in the truth of someone or something. Everyone who has ever been a follower of Jesus should be able to recall that moment when they said in their hearts, "Jesus really is who He says He is, and I trust him with everything in my past, present, and future." Biblically, this inward heart commitment is followed by a public confession and baptism. Do you remember that day when you confessed Jesus as Lord and Savior? This event is part of your story!

What is different now that you have crossed the bridge of faith?

This is where every Christ-following story becomes incredibly personal. Jesus says that the person of faith has crossed over from death to life. This transformation is the spiritual reality for everyone who believes in Jesus as the savior of their lives. According to the Bible, before salvation, we are literally dead in our sins. No matter who we are, before Jesus, we are condemned to death because of the sin in our lives. But the good news is that Jesus' death, burial, and resurrection has erased that sin and death and given us eternal life. Our lives are forever changed eternally because of this fact, and they are tangibly changed as we live out our lives on earth.

The man in John 9 said it this way, "One thing I do know. I was blind but now I see" (John 9:25). This statement was the open witness of a man who crossed over from death to life and from blindness to sight. What about you? Your unique story is the difference that Jesus has made in your life since you've crossed over by faith in Him. It has changed your family, your dreams, your work, your condition, and your outlook. The details of before and after, death and life, are your story in Christ that may encourage others to cross the same bridge that you have. Everyone has a story. What is yours?

WEEK 3: TUESDAY;
AN HISTORICAL PERSPECTIVE

JUSTIN MARTYR
AN HISTORICAL PERSPECTIVE

Justin Martyr. His last name says it all. How did he come by that moniker? Whether we have ever heard of him or not, most of us recognize the term "martyr." We think of someone who gave his/her life for Christ, even though the word originally painted a picture of a person in a courtroom who told the truth, witnessing to what he had seen and heard. If not for Justin's writings, we would know little, if anything, of his life. He was probably born in 100 AD around the time the Apostle John was dying of old age. Justin was, by far, the most eloquent defender of the faith in the second century. He was Gentile by birth, reared in Nablus, Samaria (the ancient city of Shechem), hungered for truth from a very early age, came to faith in Christ as an adult (perhaps around 130 AD), taught for a while in Ephesus, and finally moved to Rome where he continued to preach, teach, publish, and make disciples for Jesus. He loved to share his personal testimony of faith in Christ. Justin's life was marked by a passionate mastering of the Scriptures and a deep desire to teach them accurately. His Christ-centered focus was ultimately what got him into trouble with the Roman government.

The details of Justin's conversion to Christ are somewhat sketchy, but what we do know is worthy of reflection. He had been studying in several philosophical schools of the day (i.e. Stoicism and Platonism). He was particularly drawn to Plato's idea of a parallel perfect world and a transcendent Supreme Being. Justin went alone one day to the sea in order to contemplate in silence and solitude. Providentially, through a conversation on the beach with a gentle old man, he found the substance for believing in the existence of Christ. Then and there, he placed his faith in Jesus Christ. We don't know the date or circumstances that surrounded Justin's baptism, but we do know through his writings that he believed that baptism should only be undertaken after a period of thorough discipleship and preparation. He surrendered more and more of his life to Jesus, especially his mind, and his reputation grew as a defender of the faith. The pagan empire of the day was about to meet its match in Justin.

Rumors had been circulating all over the Roman Empire that Christians were cannibals and that they denied the emperor was divine. By now, Justin had opened a school of discipleship in Rome. He had written two books that he entitled *First Apology* and *Second Apology.* Some scholars suggest that Justin actually wrote a third defense of the faith, but it no longer survives. The first book described the relationship that existed between Christians and non-

Christians in the second century. Justin laid his foundation for faith in reason. The second book specifically dealt with Justin's defense against the accusations and charges leveled toward the Christian community, including the one about cannibalism. One of the most serious charges thrown at Jesus-followers of the day was a lack of intellectual weakness. Justin, and others like him, took up the challenge to engage the culture in a battle for the mind. Many pagans considered the idea of a God who was able to be, at the same time, near and far (transcendent and immanent), as absolutely unreasonable. On top of that, any notion of a resurrection from the dead was considered completely foolish (1 Corinthians 1:18-25).

Justin was widely known for his willingness to listen to those who disagreed with him. An example of this gracious form of evangelism was evident in his conversation with a Jewish man by the name of Trypho. Scholars are not in agreement on when the two day conversation actually took place, but sometime while living in Ephesus, Justin willingly entered into an extensive dialogue about being a Christian with Trypho and Trypho's friends. He treated Trypho's search for truth with great dignity and respect. In the end, Justin was reported to have offered this simple prayer: "I can wish no better thing for you, sirs, than this, that, recognizing in this way that intelligence is given to every man, you may be of the same opinion as ourselves, and believe that Jesus is the Christ of God" (Shepherd, 1998, p. 81).

Sometime around 165 AD, Justin Martyr and six of his friends were arrested and taken before the Roman magistrate. He, along with his Christian brothers, was ordered to recant faith in Christ. All of them refused to do so and were subsequently beaten, scourged, and beheaded. Justin bravely refused to accept any other lord, including the emperor, except that of His Lord and Savior, Jesus Christ. Justin Martyr, a great example of persistence and perseverance, believed that the Gospel of Jesus was intended for everyone, everywhere, regardless of wealth, nationality, race, color, gender, or creed. He saw what so many have difficulty grasping. The Good News of Jesus can cross any barrier. Those who killed Justin failed to recognize the eternal and inclusive power of the Gospel. Justin's murderers, in spite of their mocking, threats, and persecutions, did not squelch the articulate voice of Justin. He stood tall in his defense of Christ and modeled for us a prepared heart and mind ready to give reason for the hope he had (1 Peter 3:15). He stills speaks to those who will listen.

WEEK 3: WEDNESDAY;
A CROSS-CULTURAL PERSPECTIVE

THE STORY OF PASTOR BENYU

What are the five most powerful resources in our society today? If you were asked to make a list, what would you include? Allow me to take a stab. Common answers might include our military weaponry, medical advances, technological gains, the internet, democratic governments, our wealth and affluence, or even our religion. But very few, if any, would say that stories belong on that list. I'm confident that, out of a hundred people polled, none would list stories as one of the most powerful tools in our culture. And yet, the power of stories shapes people, inspires nations, transforms lives and alters the course of history time and again. Stories matter. Statistics are faceless, facts are forgotten, and arguments create division, but stories draw people in.

You have a story—a story that can shape people, transform lives, and change history. And God, in His tender mercy, stewards us thousands of opportunities to share that story. What's your story? If you were given the chance to share it, could you? If you had fifteen minutes to change someone's eternity, would you be ready? Or, better yet, would you share it? Being a good storyteller doesn't feel like a dangerous witness... but it is. Knowing your story and openly sharing it with others outlasts, outshines, and out-influences the most powerful of weapons. Let me give you an example.

Benyu was born into a Hindu family in northeast India. His family was part of the Brahmin caste, the highest caste, and he enjoyed the privilege and the esteem of the community. His father was a respected Hindu priest. Growing up, Benyu remembers watching crowds flock to his father's temple to worship their gods and to offer sacrifices. His father was faithful in teaching Benyu the family's religion and priestly duties. At a young age, Benyu was leading worship, offering sacrifices, and enjoying the privileges of authority.

To others, it seemed like Benyu embodied the epitome of success. He was the oldest son, born into a high caste family, following in his father's footsteps. People looked to him for guidance, spiritual wisdom, and connection to the gods. But they didn't know that Benyu was falling into a darkness that would consume him for years. The longer he led worship and offered sacrifices to gods he wasn't sure existed, the more conflicted he became. His life was empty. His priestly duties felt hollow. His soul withered.

The burden of leading his people down a spiritual path that he himself was unsure of was torture. Benyu turned to alcohol to cope. Every day, he would numb himself by getting drunk. It was his way of burying the questions and the doubts that continued to surface in his quieter moments. In a culture with 330 million gods, alcohol became Benyu's one true god. Over time, he became an alcoholic and, one day, found himself hospitalized with siroccos of the liver. He was drinking himself to death.

With his liver failing and his life slipping away, Benyu lay in his hospital bed alone and confused. One day, two women came into his room uninvited and asked if they could pray over him. They seemed different, but Benyu couldn't articulate what it was about them that caught his attention. After they prayed for him, they gave him a Christian gospel tract and left their contact information. Lying in his room alone that night, Benyu read about a man named Jesus for the first time. Miraculously, Benyu began to recover and to regain his health. Before long, he was discharged from the hospital with a burning desire to meet with the women who had prayed over him. He quickly set up a time to meet. They told him all about this Jesus who had healed him. They invited him to learn more, and he took them up on their offer. Benyu met weekly with them to study God's word and to learn more about Jesus.

Over the next several months, Benyu learned about the one true God, the God of Abraham, Isaac, and Jacob. He found himself overwhelmed by a God who came to give His life as a ransom for Benyu, a God who intimately wanted to experience life with Benyu and heard every one of his prayers. This was a God who sacrificed Himself once so that Benyu didn't have to continue to offer sacrifices to appease Him. One day, in response to this incredible revelation, Benyu accepted Jesus Christ as his personal Lord and Savior.

In John 5:24, Jesus reminded the crowds that whoever heard His words and believed in Him would not be condemned; in fact, they would cross over from death to life. This story was Benyu's testimony, both physically and spiritually. However, the commitment cost him everything. Benyu renounced his faith in the Hindu gods of his family and walked away from his role as a Hindu priest. Over the next several months, Benyu devoured the word and God through Bible study, correspondence courses, and local church leadership development training. He was growing in his faith and in his boldness.

Benyu is a living testimony to the power of the gospel and the truth of Jesus' words in John 5:24. He has literally crossed over from death to life, from sickness to health, his body slowly deteriorating to now being whole and healthy again. He has spiritually crossed over, leaving an empty life of idol worship to pursue the one true God as a pastor and shepherd of men. He has emotionally crossed over from a life of emptiness to a life overflowing with joy. Finally, Benyu has crossed over from an enteral separation from God to the promise of being with Him for eternity. Jesus said, whoever believes will cross over, and Benyu has done just that.

Today, Benyu is leading three separate churches. He travels from church to church teaching, preaching, and sharing the good news. He knows his story, and he shares it with anyone who will listen because within his story is the greater story that saved his life. Despite persecution and threats, he shares his story. Every morning, he awakes at 4:00am for prayer and time in the Word. He then prays with his wife and children before heading out to equip the saints and to share with the lost. When he kisses his wife good-bye, he's never guaranteed a safe return. But for a man who has already crossed over from death to life, the cost has been counted. Benyu has an incredible story, and so do you. There is power in a good story, even more so when the story is real People listen, lives are changed, and many enter into the kingdom. Jesus used stories to reach people, and so do we. What's your story? Do you know it? Are you sharing it?

WEEK 3: THURSDAY;
A LOCAL PERSPECTIVE

OPEN WITNESS: MEET JOHN ASHENFELTER

I first met John Ashenfelter in 1984 when I was a young pastor serving the Windsor Road Christian Church in Champaign, Illinois, and he was a just-as-young law student at the University of Illinois. He must have had a drink or two from the fountain of youth because John had a youthful appearance then, and nothing seems to have changed in the twenty-nine years I've known him. John's smile is infectious. He has an obvious love for Jesus that shines from the inside out. State Farm Insurance employs John as an Associate General Counsel on the company's legal team. As formidable as that role sounds, he is simply a delight to be around. His boyish charm is matched with a mature evangelist's heart. Let me introduce you to him.

How did your journey with Christ begin?

"I was thirteen years old, the youngest of six, and my family was facing a difficult time. Dad had committed adultery, but my older sisters were praying for the salvation of the family. My dad and mom were reconciled and, ten years later, became Christians. Dad passed away several years ago, but his very best day was when he said 'yes' to Jesus. I had also watched my brother share his faith with another person, so I was surrounded by faith-filled people. One of my sisters, Karon, was attending Westside Christian Church in my hometown, Springfield, Illinois, during those early years. I followed her there and began to get involved in the youth program. Responding to an altar call on September 7, 1975, I first publicly said 'yes' to Jesus."

What do you recall about your own spiritual growth?

"I've always been impressed with how God goes before us. He loves to leave the door ajar so that we can share something of our faith in Him. I've been actively involved in ECC's Upward Basketball as devotional commissioner. It has given me the opportunity of sharing over thirty half-time devotionals. All of them, in some way, get at this side of God. He's always ahead of us. Two episodes come to mind from my college days at Illinois Wesleyan. First, I was in my junior year taking a course on U.S. Criminology. I was doing an eight hour shift with one of the Peoria police officers, and a man was waiting to go to detox. He turned to me and said, 'I'm going to cut you.' I quickly began to try and calm him down, and as I look back on that potentially dangerous moment, I can see God's protection, His faithful presence, and His perfect love casting out fear. The second episode came during a domestic disturbance call during which the police officer had to separate a younger drunk from an older one. Facing horrific verbal abuse, the officer got the older one cuffed and referred to me as 'John the Father.' Suddenly settling down, the old drunk asked me, 'Are you a priest'? Without thinking, I acknowledged that I was (1 Peter 2:9), and he began to confess to me, and I had the opportunity to invite him to make confession to Christ. God is the evangelist, and He constantly goes before us.

Did you go directly from Illinois Wesleyan to the University of Illinois? What happened?

"Yes. The first year of law school was intense. The failure rate is very high. It took a toll on me. I was trying to be perfect for the sake of my family and desperately trying to please my dad. My grade average dropped significantly. I had been a straight A student at Wesleyan. Now I found myself at the U of I with a C plus average. I was devastated. Oddly, I saw God's unconditional love in my dad. He reminded me that I didn't have to continue law school if it was going to ruin me. His response spoke to me deeply of how God's perfect love covers us (Heb. 10:14). After my second year, I interned at State Farm. Providentially, I ended up back in Bloomington-Normal during the summer of 1987, studying for the bar exam and working at State Farm. I returned to ECC where I had attended in my college days. I met my wife, Liane, in 1989 while she was in a graduate program and attending ECC's New Community. We were married in 1991. It was during those early years at ECC that I began to take people through an evangelistic outreach tool called 'Peace Treaty.'" God brought a tremendous harvest through the use of that tool.

Twenty five plus years have come and gone since you returned to Bloomington-Normal, went to work at State Farm, met Liane, married, raised a family, and served in a variety of servant leader roles at ECC. What is God doing in and through you?

"It sounds crazy, but I have been an elder here since 1992. God has given me a shepherding role and a voice in our small group ministry. He has also allowed me to go on several mission trips to the Dominican Republic and Haiti. God has blessed us with two children, Elise and Zach. Elise is a better evangelist than I am. I'm constantly reminded that Jesus Christ died by our hands for our hearts. He has given me an opportunity to share with community leaders how God frees us from sin. God is regularly showing me how He opens doors for us. I have a burden to pray for those who don't know Him, the ridiculous ones, those who seem unreachable. At work, I try to model what it looks like to be in a relationship with Christ. I want my speech to be seasoned with grace. I have a visible John 3:16 plaque in my office. I constantly am looking for open doors to witness to the hope I have in Jesus (1 Peter 3:15). I think back to my involvement with Inter-Varsity Christian Fellowship in my undergraduate days and, once again, see God ahead of me, preparing me in ways that I could not have imagined. God pursues people, and He invites us into that pursuit. All God asks of us is to throw the seed, and He will reap the harvest."

John Ashenfelter strikes me as being an all-in-apprentice-to-Jesus who seeks to live his daily life as an open witness to that relationship.

WEEK 3: FRIDAY;
A PERSONAL PERSPECTIVE

There were about eight hundred people packed into an old airplane hanger in Lima, Peru, on an unforgettable night. The worship team had whipped the crowd into a sweaty lather, and the pastor was pacing around the perimeter of the room, earnestly praying and seeking some last-minute direction before taking the stage to preach. Speckled throughout the Peruvian crowd were a few dozen Minnesotan teenagers who stood out like sore thumbs in every possible way. During the final song, the pastor came to me and said, "Uno testimonio, por favor." Surprised by his spontaneity, I said, "You need a testimony right now?" Without discussion, the pastor confidently made his way to the stage to introduce the teenager who had yet to be chosen! I quickly looked at the bright, blue-eyed boy and said, "Michael, it is time for you to share your testimony. You are prepared for this!" With a deep breath and a nod of approval, Michael wove his way through the crowd to share his story.

Some of you have already felt your pulse accelerate, just thinking about Michael's situation. As my friend Doug would often say, "If you ask me to speak like that, there will be a Doug-shaped hole in the wall!" However, Michael was prepared, and God was about to use his story to communicate THE story. Our team had been "in training" for this mission trip for months. Michael, and the rest of the gang, had learned how to share a three-minute version of their stories (testimonies), and they had practiced multiple times in small groups. They had learned to share publicly three segments of a deeply personal journey toward Christ. First, Michael shared his life before becoming a Christian. Second, he shared how he transferred the leadership of his life from the reign of self to the reign of Christ. Third, he talked about his new life patterns and possibilities. Even in this unfamiliar Peruvian city, this small-town teenager was able to communicate the greatest story in history by sharing his story!

This week, we've been reminded that **everyone has a story**. Some of us will share from the platform of a stage in foreign lands. Others will share around the dinner table with wonderstruck kids. Many will share stories from cubicle to cubicle, while others will share on the fairway of a golf course. Everyone has a story, and everyone has a unique opportunity and audience afforded to them.

In our reading over the past four days, we've had the opportunity to learn about some great "witnesses" and to hear of their testimonies. Thus far we've heard:

- ◆ A Biblical Perspective from John 5:24 (Jesus teaching on authority)
- ◆ An Historical Perspective of Justin Martyr ("martyred" for his faith in 165 AD)

♦ A Cross-Cultural Perspective of Benyu (church planter in India)

♦ A Local Perspective in John Ashenfelter (Elder at Eastview Christian Church)

As we plunge into the challenging and rewarding task of expressing our own story, we thought it might be helpful to examine one more vivid example from the Apostle Paul. In Acts 26:1-29, Paul has the incredible opportunity to testify on a grand stage. It wasn't an aimless saga, nor was it a lifeless canned speech. On the contrary, it was precise, powerful, and passionate. The story is told in detail three times in the book of Acts. The first time is told in narrative form (Acts 9), and the next two are from Paul's own mouth before crowds (Acts 22 and Acts 26). Looking closely at Acts 26:1-29, we see some significant points that may be transferrable in sharing our own stories:

Paul's testimony is conveyed in three phases:

♦ First, Paul speaks of his life prior to becoming a Christian (Acts 26:1-11).

♦ Second, Paul shares a detailed account of his conversion experience (Acts 26:12-18).

♦ Third, Paul demonstrates the kind of change that has resulted from his commitment to Christ (Acts 26:19-29).

Paul's testimony is specific and focused.

♦ Paul's testimony provokes a response (see vs. 28-29).

♦ Paul's testimony glorifies God, not a sinful past.

♦ Paul's testimony demonstrates new life in Christ.

What parallels do you find between your story and Paul's story? As you consider the three phases of your story, which one would be most difficult for you to convey? I'd like to encourage you to write out your story and to craft it so that you might be prepared to share your rescue story, whether in a Peruvian hanger, in an office cubicle, or at a restaurant. Before you move on to the next segment of "OPEN," commit to at least one of the following in your personal application of an "open witness":

♦ Write your testimony. Use the simple outline noted in Acts 26 (your old life before encountering Jesus, your conversion experience, and your new life in Christ).

♦ Practice sharing your story with a trusted Christian friend.

♦ Discuss this week's reading with your small group, seeking the group's feedback and prayer support.

♦ Share your story with one of your non-Christian friends, inviting that friend to share a story as well.

John 5:24 says, "I tell you the truth, whoever hears my word and believes him who sent me has eternal life and will not be condemned; he has crossed over from death to life." Meditate on this passage, reflecting on how you've "crossed over from death to life."

WEEK 3: SATURDAY

On Saturdays throughout our study of "OPEN," we will pause to

memorize one Scripture reference and to contemplate one thought-

provoking question.

John 5:24 says, "I tell you the truth, whoever hears my
word and believes him who sent me has eternal life and
will not be condemned; he has crossed over from death to
life."

The final three words from this passage read, "death to life."

What evidence confirms that you've passed from "death to life?"

WEEK FOUR
Open To All

"Knowing and sharing the story of the Savior"

MONDAY; A BIBLICAL PERSPECTIVE

"If you are a Christ follower, then you are called, equipped, and expected to share the gospel. No exceptions!"
(Hybels, 2006, p. 61).

❖

Principle: Knowing and sharing THE STORY behind your story.

❖

"For what I received I passed on to you as of first importance: that Christ died for our sins according to the Scriptures, that he was buried, that he was raised on the third day according to the Scriptures." I Corinthians 15:3&4

I am a retired little league football coach. From the time my youngest son, Caleb, was old enough to play, you could find me every fall, four nights a week, on the practice field, whistle around my neck, surrounded by seven, eight, and nine-year-old boys. Aside from the many humorous moments (the oversized helmets and shoulder pads made most of them look like football bobble heads), I truly enjoyed the chance to form and to teach these young men in the basics of the game. Was I a good coach? Well, it depends on what you mean by "good." We lost some and won some, but I did form some great relationships with kids who are now grown men. But my most important accomplishment was to lay the foundation for every football game they would ever play.

You see, in beginner football, there's really not a whole lot of strategy and "coaching" going on. Coaching these young guys is not about wins and losses; it's about teaching them to play the game the right way. My goal each year was to teach these boys three simple basics: 1) How to tackle 2) How to block 3) How to move as a team at the same time. Without these three skills, no physical ability, game plan, or coaching strategy in the world will work. Success, at this level, was a game in which each team member could tackle the other guy with the ball, block when his teammate had the ball, and perform all in sync when the ball was snapped. These are the most important skills in football. I was a successful coach if I taught every boy on my team to do these three things well.

The Christian faith, like football, has some basics, some "most important" aspects that every Christ follower should know and be able to articulate. Theology can be very complex, but it's not complicated. In Paul's first letter to the believers at Corinth, he passes on the simple truths essential to faith in Jesus. These truths that had been passed on to Paul are not only foundational to our faith, but also crucial to sharing the story of Christ with those around us.

It is interesting to note that many scholars confirm that these verses in Corinthians serve as one of the first creeds of the early church. A creed is simply a statement or saying about what one believes that is often repeated by those who adhere to it. Because Paul became a Christian about two years after the church had begun, he had to be taught the basics. This early statement of faith was likely recited by Christians as early as 35 A.D., making it the earliest known creed of Jesus' church. Paul passed this statement of beliefs on to the Corinthians and all the churches he ministered to.

One word of this creed is rather important here. Paul uses the Greek word *protos* to describe the faith statement he was passing on. We translate the Greek into "first importance" because this word means "that which comes first" (as in the first thing in a sequence), but it also means "first in priority." In other words, according to the Bible, the death, burial, and resurrection of Jesus are the most important truths we have to believe and to share about our faith.

Christ died for our sins

The good news of the Christian message begins with a sacrifice for sins. The Bible teaches that "all have sinned and fall short of the glory of God" (Romans 3:23). The word also states that the "wages of sin is death" (Romans 6:23). Human history and current headlines give testimony to the reality that every man is prone to the destructive acts of sin. Only Christianity offers a solution for this problem. Try as they might, many religions offer rules, gods, philosophies, rituals, and solutions, but they are unsuccessful because, through them, man can't fix his condition or pay for his sin. So God sent a savior. He sent his son Jesus to do the work of salvation by his death on the cross. Yet, the story doesn't end with a cold corpse in a dark burial cave. Jesus didn't stay dead.

He was raised on the third day

The historical resurrection of Jesus is the most important event in all human history and the most important teaching of Christianity. It's the most important human event because it addresses each of our realities. Each of our lives will end in death, and there is absolutely nothing any of us can do about it. So, when someone follows the human reality of death by living again, we should pay attention to that person. Along with this miracle, the resurrection becomes the most important teaching of the Christian faith because Jesus promised he would come back to life and that, in so doing, he would give us eternal life. While attending the funeral of a close friend, Jesus speaks of the resurrection in this way: "I am the resurrection and the life. He who believes in me will live, even though he dies; and whoever lives and believes in me will never die" (John 11:25-26). These basics are a part of the most important story, and it did not occur by chance.

This story occurred according to God's plan

The Scriptures reveal God's will and plan for human kind, and the death, burial, and resurrection of Jesus was his plan all along. In the Old Testament, God spoke by His Spirit through prophets who recorded these words to preserve them for future Christians. These are the Scriptures that Paul references in the early church creed. These are the Old Testament Scriptures that pointed to the coming of a savior long before Jesus was born! This means that God always had a plan to take away our sins and to give us life because he was talking about it way before Christ arrived. The whole Bible points to these two realities through the person of Jesus. Isaiah 53 speaks of Jesus being "crushed for our iniquities" and tells us that, "by his wounds we are healed." In the prophet Hosea, we find a reference to life after death, which Jewish scholars interpreted to be the resurrection of the Christ (see Hosea 6:2). God has always had a plan to save the world. That's what Jesus said in John 3:17 when talking with Nicodemus: "God did not send his son into the world to condemn the world, but to save the world through him."

These are the basics of THE STORY. This early statement of faith contains the basic knowledge that each of us needs in order to share the good news of Jesus. You may not be able to discuss all theological teaching from the Bible, but if you understand these three, you can share THE STORY. There are other parts to share, but these are the first aspects, the most important facts, and now that you know, I pray you will share them soon.

WEEK 4: TUESDAY;
An Historical Perspective

Scillitan Martyrs
An Historical Perspective

Since childhood, I have wondered what being a martyr for Jesus would be like. Maybe other children contemplated the same mystery. I don't know. I never, ironically, had the courage to ask. I imagined bravely standing in front of a firing squad at sunrise, refusing the blindfold. I could see myself at high noon positioned next to the hangman's noose and being asked, "Do you have any final words?" and then saying, "I believe in Jesus. I will not recant." I would dream of being forced to kneel on a bloody tree stump in front of a screaming crowd and have the razor-sharp sword drawn by the executioner while the blade reflected the last rays of dusk's light. I pondered what it would be like to have your name printed in bold type on the front of the local newspaper: "Pastor Dies for His Faith." I know it can sound self-serving and immature. Sometimes, my childhood fantasies got the best of me. I say all of that because I wish with all my heart that all of us knew more about those who have rejected the easy way and refused to deny Christ and were martyred. The Scillitan Martyrs come to mind.

These twelve North African Christians, seven men and five women, from a place called Scilla (or Scillium) were tried, found guilty, and executed under the reign of the Roman emperor, Marcus Aurelius, and the proconsul, Saturninus, July 17, 180 AD, in Carthage. The details of their story are somewhat sketchy. However, some of the pieces of the story are recorded in a document called *The Acts of the Scillitan Martyrs*. This record is considered the earliest document of the church of Africa. The names of the twelve recorded in *The Acts* are Speratus, Nartzalus, Cintinus, Veturius, Felix, Aquilinus Laetantius Januaria, Generosa, Vestia, Donata, and Secunda. Speratus, the first listed, appears to be the spokesman for the entire group. The document is shaped in the form of a legal brief. It begins with the date and the names of the accused. The most helpful part of *The Acts* is the court transcripts that give us the actual conversation that ensued between Speratus and the Roman accusers. The conversation went as follows.

> **Saturninus, the proconsul:** "You can win the indulgence of our lord the Emperor, if you return to a sound mind."

> **Speratus:** "We have never done ill, we have not given ourselves to wrong, we have never spoke ill, but when ill-treated we have given thanks; because we pay heed to OUR EMPEROR."

> **Saturninus:** "We too are religious, and our religion is simple, and we swear by the genius of our lord the Emperor, and pray for his welfare, as you also ought to do."

Speratus: "If you will peaceably lend me your ears, I can tell you the mystery of simplicity."

Saturninus: "I will not lend my ears to you, when you beg to speak evil things of our sacred rites, but rather swear by the genius of our lord the Emperor."

Speratus: "I don't recognize the empire of this world; but rather I serve God, whom no man has seen, nor with his eyes can see. I have committed no theft; but if I have bought anything I pay the tax; because I know my Lord, the King of kings and Emperor of all nations."

Donata: (one of the accused) "Honor to Caesar as Caesar, but fear to God."

Vestia: (one of the accused) "I am a Christian."

Secunda: (one of the accused) "What I am, that I wish to be."

Saturninus to Speratus: "Do you persist in being a Christian?"

Speratus: "I am a Christian." (All the accused agreed)

Saturninus: "What are the things in your satchel?"

Speratus: "Books and letters of Paul, a just man."

Saturninus: "I offer you a delay of thirty days in order to think this matter over."

Speratus: "I am a Christian." (All the accused agreed)

Saturninus, the proconsul, then read out the decree from the tablet: "Speratus, Nartzalus, Cittinus, Donata, Vestia, Secunda and the rest having confessed that they live according to the Christian rite, since after opportunity offered them of returning to the custom of the Romans they have obstinately persisted, it is determined they be put to the sword."

Speratus: "We give thanks to God."

Nartzalus: (one of the accused) "Today we are martyrs in heaven; thanks be to God."

Saturninus: "Let it be declared by the herald: Speratus, Nartzalus, Cittinus, Veturius, Felix, Aquilinus, Laetantius, Januaria, Generosa, Vestia, Donata, and Secunda, I have ordered to be executed."

The brief exchange between the Roman proconsul and these courageous Christ-followers models for us in succinct form what it means to know and to share the sufferings of Jesus (Philippians 3:10). Some unknown Christian later added the following words to this court scene: "And so they all together were crowned with martyrdom; and they reign with the Father and the Son and the Holy Ghost, forever and ever. Amen." The example of the Scillitan Martyrs is not a glamorization or glorification of Christian death; rather, it is a vivid testimony to what the love of Christ and His grace can empower anyone to do. After all, even if we surrender our bodies to the flames, "but have not love," we gain nothing (1 Corinthians 13:3). The love of Christ makes all the difference. His love can cause the most hesitant among us to take a stand to share the story of our Savior.

WEEK 4: WEDNESDAY;
A CROSS-CULTURAL PERSPECTIVE

THE TESTIMONY OF DIWAS

Paul reminds us in Romans 1:16 that the good news of Jesus con-tains the power of God to bring salvation to *everyone*. That really screwed things up for the religious elite in Jesus' day. These religious leaders had worked really hard to create a religious system from which they benefitted. Their disciplined lifestyle and devotion to their faith was commended by many, but they totally missed the point. Jesus reserved his harshest criticisms and condemnations for those "religious" guys. He revealed to them that they were missing what actually mattered to God while protecting traditions (Mark 7:8). The problem was that they expended so much effort loving them-selves that they had nothing left for God or neighbor. Jesus passion-ately called his people to re-focus upward on the Father and outward to neighbors. He was calling them back to a way of life in which all people could come to the Father. Jesus was open to all people from all walks of life. He calls us to know and to share his story with all people. Let me introduce you to a man who has given his life to knowing and to sharing the story. His life is spent equipping others to know and to share the story.

Diwas was born into a Buddhist family in northeast India. His hometown is tucked away in the foothills of the Himalaya mountain range. When Diwas was growing up, his family would often spend time together at the local Buddhist monastery. His father made sure that Diwas and his brother were brought up to know the tenets of their faith and the spiritual practices of their family.

One day, when Diwas was in high school, his younger brother began to have strange nightmares that quickly turned into night terrors. In them, he was chased and abducted by Buddhist monks from the monastery. Over time, the attacks increased in frequency and severity and began to manifest themselves in physical ways. It became evident that the family had opened themselves to demonic influence through idol worship. Diwas' brother was tormented day and night. He was attacked mentally, physically, emotionally, and spiritually. Over time, he stopped eating. He became bed ridden, and, slowly, his body, mind, and soul began to atrophy. Despite everything they tried, he couldn't escape the oppression.

Desperate for answers, Diwas' family enlisted the help of several Buddhist leaders in the community. They prayed over him, but nothing changed. As his condition continued to deteriorate, the family enlisted the help of local witch doctors. They prayed over him and performed ceremonies, but nothing changed. He continued to slip farther and farther into himself and farther away from his family and this life.

One day, Christians from the neighboring village asked Diwas' family if they could pray for his brother. Fearing they would lose him soon, the family decided that they had nothing to lose. The believers came to pray, and Diwas remembered thinking it strange that they didn't ask for compensation, relics, or other objects from the family. They simply prayed. They prayed in the name of Jesus. They entered his brother's room and only stayed for ten minutes. Then they left. Nothing happened. Diwas and his family went to sleep hopeless but, in the morning, were shocked to hear his brother ask for food. He was hungry. He also asked for someone to read the Bible that was left for him. Slowly, over time, as the family read God's word together, he regained his appetite and his strength, and his night terrors disappeared.

In response to his brother's healing, Diwas accepted Christ. After graduating from high school, Diwas decided to spend his life serving the Lord. He would go on to get his Masters of Divinity degree at a seminary in southern India. It was at that time that he was approached by CICM about helping to launch a biblical training academy in northeast India. This academy would train future church planters who would go to the surrounding cities, villages, and countries with the gospel. These young men would plant churches in some of the most dangerous places in the world. CICM wasn't promising Diwas riches or notoriety; in fact, he would be living in a dorm with twenty-five young men. He would have to cook alongside them in a makeshift outdoor kitchen. He would have limited privacy but also the opportunity to pour his heart and soul into these young men. Diwas quickly agreed.

Today, Diwas is the Director of the CICM Biblical Academy in Darjeeling, India. Founded in 2009, this academy has already trained and sent over forty church planters and pastors to the surrounding countries of Tibet, Nepal, Bangladesh, Myanmar, Bhutan, and Northern India. Diwas continues to sacrifice so that many can know the story and be trained to share it with others. As Director of the academy, he lives in a space smaller than many college dorm rooms. He was recently married, and his wife lives in a neighboring town where she's a teacher. Though married, Diwas is committed to training, coaching, and teaching these men while sharing his life with them. He only sees his wife on the weekends. Why? Because knowing and sharing the story of the Savior, and training others to do the same, is worth everything to Diwas.

Ask yourself if knowing and sharing the story is that important to you. What length, what sacrifice, what ridicule, are we, the body of

Eastview Christian Church, willing to endure together so that more will know the Savior? As we challenge each other to give more, one day we'll stand at eternity's gate together, alongside brothers like Diwas, knowing there was nothing else worth giving our lives for.

WEEK 4: THURSDAY;
A Local Perspective

Open to All: Meet Jessica Bockman

Jessica, Jess for short, is a senior student at Illinois State University, with a major in Interpersonal Communications and a minor in Sociology. We met between classes for a breakfast chat at Merry Ann's Café not far from the campus center. Jess is plenty busy. However, it is not her studies that define her but, rather, her relationship with Jesus Christ. Ironically, this bright, joy-filled, and effervescent young lady with a smile that could melt ice in Glacier National Park struggled with school. Her early years of education found Jess diagnosed with a learning disability and ultimately enrolled in a private Christian school. The truth is that Jessica has faced plenty of challenges in her twenty-something years of life. First, she did not grow up in the church. Some people might consider that fact a blessing, but Jess knows better. Second, her father battles Alzheimer's and faces the continual side effects of being an alcoholic. Third, and in no way the end of the story, Jess has experienced family life that has not always been supportive of her Jesus-following commitment. This Ft. Wayne, Indiana, girl is a devoted disciple of Jesus Christ. Here's how our conversation went.

Name some of your spiritual mile markers. How did you meet Jesus?

"I admit mom and dad spoiled me. I have two older brothers, and I'm the baby. Even before I knew who God was, I would pray to Him. There was lots of seed-planting going in my life in those early childhood years. Confirmation class was helpful, though not personal. Going to church played a part in my formation as well. Religion class at the Lutheran school I attended was foundational for me in terms of knowing facts and stories from Scripture, but not in terms of a personal relationship with Jesus. It was when I came to ISU that the most significant spiritual mile marker took place."

Tell me about that. What happened at ISU?

"My Uncle Dave helped make the way for me to attend ISU. I came to campus in 2009. I didn't know anyone. My cheerleading experience in high-school was where I found my self-esteem and that was no longer a part of my life. I had brought a devotional book from home, and I read it faithfully for the first few weeks of the fall semester, but I was not yet reading the Bible. I rushed for sorority, thinking that would be a cool thing to do, but God had other plans for me. I providentially met two female students who invited me to attend ECC's Fuel ministry. The very same week I was invited to join a sorority, I was also invited to attend Fuel. How crazy is that? I ended up attending a retreat at Lake Williamson and not joining that sorority. My whole course of life shifted. If I could create an image of what my life had been like up to that point, I would describe someone with closed fists. The sermons and worship time at that retreat marked my life. I opened my heart through literally opening my hands, and I gave my life to Jesus. I was baptized the next day at the camp. I started attending Bible study and asking God to use me."

What's difficult about sharing Jesus' story intertwined with your story at ISU?

"Christianity, from a lot of perspectives, can seem like fitting a square peg into a round hole. Christian faith is the square peg, and ISU is the round hole. Some well-meaning Christians drive other non-Christians away from the Lord by giving off the impression that you must be a certain kind of person or act a certain way *before* accepting Christ. I try to genuinely love people with the same love Christ has shown me. For example, one night I was driving on campus, and I saw a girl waiting for a bus. I pulled over the car and asked her, 'Do you need a ride?' She did, and I ended up driving her to Waterson Towers. She asked me, 'Where are you coming from?' She had spotted my Bible on the dashboard of my car. I told her, 'I'm coming from Bible Study.' We ended up talking for over two hours. I listened as she opened up about her struggles in life and frustrations with Christianity. I was able to share Scripture with her and how I had seen God working in similar circumstances in my life. I ended up inviting her to Fuel, and, a year later, my discipler and I got the opportunity to baptize her! There are so many students in need of the new life Jesus provides."

What breaks your heart at ISU?

Students that have never heard the Good News break my heart. They only know of one way to live, one idea, one picture of life, and that life has failed to grasp or to meet God's love. God has given me a personality of boldness. It is a blessing and a curse, but He does use it. I simply befriend people and try to love them the way Jesus does. I use my story to build a bridge to each person."

What do you watch for at ISU?

"I look for opportunity and allow God to position me to walk through the doors He opens. I am particularly aware of people who are alone. I'm a college student, and so are they. It's that simple. I look for common experiences and ask questions like, 'What motivates you? What major are you? How are you doing?' If that flops, I try again. I'm not afraid to make myself look awkward. So often, I have discovered that the other person is desperate for a conversation.'"

Now you know Jessica Bockman just a little better. She truly believes that God has created us with eternity in our hearts (Ecclesiastes 3:11) and invites us to partner with Him in knowing and sharing the story of Jesus.

WEEK 4: FRIDAY;
A PERSONAL PERSPECTIVE

Every once in a while, my repressed feisty nature comes out to play. This alter ego has been known to take over when my favorite team is losing, when I'm sleep deprived, when I'm hungry, or when I see an opportunity to capitalize on a teachable moment. On rare occasions, this feisty nature prompts me to *manufacture* the moment rather than just wait for it to happen!

About ten years ago, I was in an airport, waiting in line for a forgettable meal between flights. In front of me was a group of students all wearing the same bright t-shirts adorned with their youth ministry logo and a catchy phrase about "missions." In a flash, my feisty nature took over, and I began to read the shirts aloud. The two students nearest to me overheard my monologue and turned around with a wave of enthusiasm. I began to ask a variety of questions:

Me: What's up with the shirts?
Students: We're coming back from a missions trip!
Me: Wait a second ... You aren't "Christians" are you?
Students: Yes we are!
Me: You're kidding. You actually believe all that stuff?
Students: Yeah, we really do ...
Me: You mean to tell me you believe that the Bible is trustworthy? That God (who we've never seen) sent His Son to

die for something we apparently did wrong? That Jesus
rose from the dead? ...

By this time, one of the students had abandoned his friend and headed for the hills! The remaining student dug in his heels and began to answer the combative and cynical guy in front of him. After several more critical questions and some courageous answers, I revealed that I completely agreed with him, that I was just curious to see if he would stand strong in the face of opposition ... and that I was a pastor on a missions trip myself! His response: "Man you make a good atheist"! He literally gasped and placed his hands on his knees, bewildered by the outcome of this bizarre interaction. The student who had retreated from the conversation quickly re-engaged, and I spent several minutes laughing with them and encouraging them in their ability to articulate their faith and to stand firm in the face of opposition. Shockingly, I even received a warm reception from the youth pastor of that missions team once he heard of my antics!

The story of this encounter is fun to share, but it also serves as a reminder that there are times when we need more than a clever t-shirt or an affiliation with a church. As Christ followers, we are expected to know and to share, not just our story, but how it intersects with THE story. The "Great Commission" (Matthew 28:18-20) was not intended only for a small band of first century disciples. It was intended for me, for you, and for all who will call on the name of Jesus as Lord and Savior. The heartbeat of Jesus' words in John 3:16-17 is a wide-sweeping invitation (to the world) by very precise means (through Christ).

You and I are uniquely designed to reach our circles of influence with the life-changing, eternity-altering message of the Gospel. The great news is that we get to communicate this great message in a style as unique as the messengers! Looking again at the testimony in Acts 26, we see that Paul emphasized foundational and timeless truth with his own personal flair. A closer look at verse 23 will help us to see how three essential elements of our faith are addressed concisely and compellingly (compare/contrast with 1 Corinthians 15:3, 4 and Monday's devotional for this week).

That the Christ Would Suffer: There is no shortage of passages that proclaim the suffering that our Savior would endure on our behalf. From the initial prophecy of Genesis 3:15 to the intricate detail of Isaiah 53, Jesus' suffering has been foretold. From the mouth of John the Baptist, we hear Him called "the Lamb of God" (John 1:29, 36). Isaiah refers to Jesus as a "man of sorrows," knowing hardship and grief (Isaiah 53:3). Christ Himself would anticipate His suffering on the cross (Mark 10:45). Ultimately, this suffering provides the "great exchange" whereby our sins are taken on by Christ, and

His righteousness is taken on by those who place their trust in Him (Romans 5:6-9).

As the First to Rise from the Dead: Christ's work did not end on the cross. Paul mentions in 1 Corinthians 15:12-22 that the resurrection of Jesus is absolutely essential. In Romans 6:3-11, Paul passionately argues that we follow Christ, not only in new Kingdom values and vision, but in death and resurrection. Our baptism demonstrates the burial of the old self and a resurrection that invites "a new life." As with all other things, our Great Teacher has modeled what His students must do.

He Would Proclaim Light to Both Our people and the Gentiles: The same God who said, "Let there be light" (Genesis 1:3) also said, "I am the light of the world" (John 8:12). This great "illumination" is offered, not just to the Jews, but to all who would place their faith in Christ. As we've noted throughout this week's teaching, THE story (God's story of redemption) is "open to all" who would willingly participate.

This week's reading has taken us on a journey through the following perspectives:

♦ A Biblical Perspective from 1 Corinthians 15:1-6 (Paul teaching on matters of "first importance")

♦ An Historical Perspective of the Scillitan Martyrs (North African Christians, 180 A.D.)

◆ A Cross-Cultural Perspective of Diwas (staff member of CICM)

◆ A Local Perspective in Jessica Bockman (ISU student at Eastview Christian Church)

These stories are intended to inspire you to consider the magnitude of the message of Christ and the means by which we can personally participate in connecting *our story* with *THE STORY*. Now that we've covered some of the essential elements of this message, commit to one or more of the following this week:

◆ Ask God to reveal any hesitancy you may have toward certain people groups. Are there any people you've unnecessarily screened from the Gospel?

◆ Discuss this week's reading with your small group, seeking the group's feedback and prayer support for you further to develop a heart that is "open to all."

◆ Develop and practice sharing an outline that conveys your story as a part of THE STORY. Include at least one Scripture reference.

◆ John 3:16-17 says, "For God so loved the world that he gave his one and only Son, that whoever believes in him shall not perish but have eternal life. For God did not send his Son into the world to condemn the world, but to save the world through him." Reflect on this grand invitation and the means by which it is received.

WEEK 4: SATURDAY

On Saturdays throughout our study of "OPEN," we will pause to memorize one Scripture reference and to contemplate one thought-provoking question.

> John 3:16-17 says, "For God so loved the world that he gave his one and only Son, that whoever believes in him shall not perish but have eternal life. For God did not send his Son into the world to condemn the world, but to save the world through him."

God's love for the world went beyond a passive feeling to an active sharing. In His case, He shared the greatest gift of all time (the life of His Son, Jesus). How will you join God in sharing His Son with others?

WEEK FIVE
OPEN MOUTH

"TIMELY TRUTH-TELLING"

MONDAY; A BIBLICAL PERSPECTIVE

---

*"A good witness is like a signpost. It doesn't matter whether
it is old, young, pretty, ugly; it has to point the right direction
and be able to be understood.
We are witnesses to Christ, we point to him" (White, 1976, n.p.).*
❖
Principle: Share the good news when the opportunity arises.
❖
*"...do not worry beforehand about what to say. Just say whatever
is given you at the time, for it is not you speaking,
but the Holy Spirit" (Mark 13:11).*

You never know when you will find yourself in the middle of a

conversation about God. It happens to me all of the time. Admittedly,

I have more opportunities than most due to the fact that I'm a pastor.

Over the years, I have been drawn into theological discussions in a

wide variety of social settings. Many of these conversations begin with the usual pleasantries and greetings, but they inevitably move to questions about what I do for a living. When I reveal that I am a pastor, the conversation suddenly shifts to God stuff. Honestly, I consider it an easy way to get people talking about Jesus—a sort of built-in spiritual pick-up line. In these instances, God supplies the opportunity, and I talk about His Son.

One such opportunity came several years ago on a flight from Colorado back to my home in Normal, IL. I had just spoken at a youth conference and was preparing for my sermon the next day, so my Bible was open, and I was reviewing my notes. I had simply acknowledged the lady seated next to me with a, "Hello, how are you?" but had no intentions to continue a dialogue. The Holy Spirit had other ideas. She began, "You must be a preacher." I answered that I was. Before I could return to my review, she continued, "I guess you probably don't think too much of my kind then, huh?" I am often slow, but even I could see that God had ordained this moment, so I closed my Bible, looked at her, and responded, "your kind?"

She quickly revealed that she was a lesbian who was flying home to visit her dying mother. Seriously, it was that fast! Where do I begin? What should I say? Even a preacher wonders what to say next. So many ideas flashed through my spirit. I wanted to speak the truth in love. I wanted to turn the conversation to Jesus. I wanted to convey to her that I love "her kind" and all kinds. I wanted to minister to her in this tough time in her life. But, alas, I wasn't prepared for this conversation. I didn't plan on it happening, and I didn't know what I would say. So, I opened my mouth and prayed that the Holy Spirit would do the rest, and by the grace of God, He did an incredible work.

In the second gospel, Mark records some of Jesus' warnings and instructions to his followers concerning the last days. He predicted that they would face physical persecution for their faith ("you will be...flogged in the synagogues" Mark 13:9). He warned them that they would be arrested and brought to trial before pagan government officials (see Mark 13:11). In other words, they would get to speak many times for Jesus, and they would speak this message to the some of the most influential people in the world. It's true that these would not consist of comfortable chances to share their faith, but they would have plenty of preaching opportunities

This passage in Mark (13:9-11) introduces three preaching words that help us understand exactly what these "open mouth" appointments would be, and they also serve to guide us in our Jesus conversations. The first word is "witnesses," which comes from the Greek word *martureo*—a word that means to tell your testimony or story (what you know). We have also noted that our English word "martyr" comes from believers being killed because of their stories.

The second word is "gospel," and that word comes from the Greek *euangelion* , literally meaning "well message" or "good news." Ultimately, every time we open our mouths to speak of Jesus, we have good news to share. Most of us are not called to debate theology, to defend the Bible, or to prove the existence of God, but we are all called to tell the good news of Jesus. Jesus tells his followers that the good news must be preached to all nations—and we are the preachers!

Finally, we come to the word "preached." This word in the original language is *karusso*, and, originally, it had to do with proclaiming news in an official capacity. This action was often associated with heralds who would come to town and make royal proclamations. In our vernacular, preaching is often associated with the person who speaks from the Bible on Sunday mornings in church. While this interpretation is preaching and the church does need these kinds of preachers, the Bible teaches us that we are all preachers--proclaimers of God's message of grace in a variety of settings.

How do you prepare for these "open mouth" occasions? You don't. According to Jesus' teaching in Mark 13:11, you just start talking. Christians often get so worried, anticipating the sequence of potential questions, conversational turns, and faith roadblocks that will jeopardize their witnessing opportunities. We should realize "it is not you speaking, but the Holy Spirit." We just need to open our mouths and to let the Spirit do His thing. He has been pointing to Jesus from the beginning of human history. Stick with the basics. Begin with your testimony of what Jesus has done for you, share the good news of His saving love and grace, and boldly proclaim it as a representative of God. You'll be surprised by what the Spirit says through you!

As for the lady on the plane, I wish I could tell you that I prayed a prayer of faith and repentance with her. I wish I could tell you that we deplaned, and I baptized her in the terminal fountain as strangers wept and sang hymns. Well, that didn't happen, but God did afford me an opportunity. He did give me a story to share. And He did give me good news. The point is that I opened my mouth, and that's really all He needs from me!

WEEK 5: TUESDAY;
AN HISTORICAL PERSPECTIVE

PERPETUA
AN HISTORICAL PERSPECTIVE

Persecution of Christians began shortly after the resurrection of Christ. Even a simple reading of Acts will verify the truth of that statement. Most of that anti-Christian sentiment came initially from the Jewish leaders in and around Jerusalem. Eventually, the Roman government, especially in the city of Rome, under Nero's reign (54-68 AD), began to practice a localized persecution. Paul and Peter were both martyred during this period. Later, during Domitian's rule (81-96 AD), persecution against Christians became more wide spread. When Marcus Aurelius came to power (161-180 AD), a spirit of opposition against Christianity was strong, especially in areas where faith in Christ seemed to flourish like that of North Africa. During this time lived a beautiful and intelligent woman of noble birth, Perpetua, raised in a supportive family, surrounded with great wealth, and given educational opportunities that few would have enjoyed. This woman came to the conclusion that "whatever was to *her* profit, *she* now considered loss for the sake of Christ...*She* consider them rubbish, that *she* might gain Christ" (Philippians 3:7-8). How Perpetua became a Jesus-follower is uncertain. Like the Scillitan Martyrs we've already studied, she grew up in North Africa, a strong and vibrant center of active and courageous Christian faith, during the last part of the second century and the first part of the third century AD. Four Roman emperors sat on the throne during this period (193-211 AD), Pertinax, Didius Julianus, Septimius Severus, along with co-emperor Caracalla. These were troubling times in so many ways.

Perpetua, in her early twenties, was newly married and a mother of an infant son. She had been arrested along with her servant, Felicitas, and several other Christians. Because she kept a diary of her experiences, we have a firsthand glimpse into her martyrdom. According to her diary entries and the subsequent entries of those who witnessed her experience, Perpetua had been confronted by her father to give into the authorities and to renounce her faith in Christ. Her response was eloquent and direct: "Father, do you see this vase here?" "Yes," he replied. She asked, "Could this be called by any other name than what it is?" "No," he said. "Well, so too I cannot be called anything other than what I am, a Christian," was her response. Because of her imprisonment and her ongoing study and preparation to be immersed into Christ, Perpetua had not yet been baptized. It was while she was waiting for her sentencing that she asked to be immersed. It is beyond amazing that the authorities granted her request. She was given permission to nurse her baby until her hearing, but, ultimately, he was taken from her as a means to leverage her rejection of Christ. She refused.

Her family, especially her father, continued to plead with her to declare allegiance to the emperor and to deny Christ. On the day of her hearing, the Roman proconsul, Hilarianus, said to her, "Have pity on your father's grey head; have pity on your infant son. Offer the sacrifice for the welfare of the emperors." "I will not," she retorted. "Are you a Christian?" the governor inquired. "Yes, I am," was her bold reply. She was thrown to the ground, beaten, and then sentenced to die in the arena. Perpetua, on the day of her execution, was stripped naked, bundled in a large net along with the other condemned Christians, and dragged into the stadium where an enormous crowd had gathered. Wild beasts and gladiators were present to carry out the death sentences. A wild heifer charged the group and tossed Perpetua into the air. Her servant, Felicitas, had been crushed, so Perpetua made her way toward her sister in Christ and helped her up on her feet. They stood side by side while a leopard was let loose. Bloodied and battered, Perpetua, Felicitas, and the others were lined up and then killed by the gladiator's sword. Apparently the gladiator was young and inexperienced and didn't kill Perpetua with his initial thrust. She took his trembling hand, modeling the love of Christ, and guided it to her own throat. This brave disciple of Jesus, along with her fellow believers, was killed March 7, 203 AD.

It is almost incomprehensible to us twenty-first century Christians to imagine the gore and violence of Perpetua's kind of death. Felicitas, her co-martyr, had just given birth to a child! The crowd that had screamed for blood earlier now saw the milk dripping from her breasts and was suddenly horrified. What kind of hatred has to be summoned in order, not only to kill someone because of her belief in the life, death, burial, and resurrection of Jesus Christ, but to torture her because she does not adhere to a particular worldview? Man's inhumanity to man has existed since Cain killed Abel. Even Christians, in the name of Christ, have committed acts of violence, terror, and murder. None of this hatred resembles the life that Jesus offers. The Jesus-following life is a call to continual submission to His way, not ours. What is so strikingly beautiful about stories like Perpetua's is the literal way they model for us a steadfastness to "love *our* enemies and pray for those who persecute *us*, that *we* may be sons *and daughters* of *our* Father in heaven" (Matthew 5:44-45). This week's theme, Open Mouth: Praying to be Fearless, can be our constant prayer and our perpetual reminder that only the love of Christ makes it possible for us to love the unloving.

WEEK 5: WEDNESDAY;
A Cross-Cultural Perspective

THE TESTIMONY OF TIHARU

At a young age, Tiharu's mother died, leaving his father, a common laborer, to raise Tiharu and his seven sisters. His father earned around $.75 cents a day. His daily wage wasn't enough to provide food for his children. The family began to slip farther and farther into debt until, one day, Tiharu's father was forced to do the unthinkable. As he sat Tiharu down, with tears in his eyes, he told his son that he was selling him to a farmer as a slave hand. If he didn't, they would all starve. The price that was paid for Tiharu was a five-pound bag of rice to feed his siblings. Tiharu begged his father not to do it, pleading, "Father, I want to do something with my life." But it soon came to pass; Tiharu was sold as a child slave.

At the age of seven, Tiharu loved school. He loved learning and cried at the thought of having to drop out, but he was forced to leave behind everything he knew. He was now responsible for taking care of his master's herd of forty cattle. The man was ruthless. Tiharu worked long hours, usually twelve hours a day and was often beaten or tortured for not "doing good enough work." On his good days, his pay was a bowl of rice and lentils. This precious child of God had no voice. He was stuck in an abusive environment through no fault of his own. He was a lost child among the millions in India forced into human trafficking. He was on the verge of becoming just another statistic. His life was over before it ever started.

Take a moment to think about what your life was like when you were seven years old. Close your eyes, and, just for a moment, remember. For the majority of us, it was filled with school, friends, some sort of stable home life and dreams of what the future would hold. There was a beautiful innocence. To get a little more personal, think about your children or grand-children around that age and the beauty and innocence they possessed. Now, try to image them being ripped away, sold into an abusive environment, and having to forfeit everything their tiny hearts had hoped and dreamed for. What a horrific and hopeless situation. But not with God. With God all things are possible. Little did Tiharu know that his life was about to take another unexpected turn. When he pleaded with his earthly father "I want to do something with my life" he had no idea what his heavenly father had in store.

One day, a CICM pastor working in the area heard about Tiharu's story and approached his father. CICM's children's program could buy Tiharu back. CICM would pay Tiharu's ransom and provide the funds for his schooling and the family's food shortages as well. Soon, Tiharu was reunited with his family and back in school. He was rescued from the abuse of his earthly master and experienced the redemptive love of Jesus Christ, his heavenly master. He accepted Jesus as his Lord and Savior. As Tiharu grew, he never forgot what those lonely nights on the ranch were like. As he grew in stature, so did his passion to help others the way he had been helped. His passion to share the good news of Jesus Christ with others grew as well.

As a young man, Tiharu decided to attend the CICM biblical academy in Damoh, India. He was trained in theology, preaching, and church planting. At the time of his graduation, Tiharu had grown into a fearless preacher and leader. God had transformed this seven-year-old child slave with no voice into a young man with a booming voice and a million-dollar smile. With his studies complete and his calling sure, it was time to go home to the villages of his youth.

Tiharu began to spend every day traveling to share the good news with people. His voice was a powerful presence within the surrounding villages, and people gathered to hear Tiharu's story. His unwavering confidence and robust voice captured their hearts. Today, Tiharu has planted five churches, and he continues to pastor and to preach in all of them. He has also baptized over 3,000 people. You would have to baptize one person every day for the next 8.5 years to reach that goal. Tiharu also carries in him a passion to redeem the voiceless. This little boy, who once didn't have a voice, now stands in the gap for those who can't save themselves. Tiharu has personally rescued over 150 children out of slavery. Little boys and girls with dreams and aspirations like him, little boys and girls who cry out like Tiharu, "I want to do something with my life," their stories are still being written, and so is yours.

We might be tempted to shy away from Tiharu's story. Instead of inspiring us, it could cause some of us to say, "God could never use me in that way," as we dismiss the possibility. But let's not be so quick to limit what God could do through the life of just one dangerous witness. God can use us, right here in Bloomington, Normal, to do the miraculous if we'll let him. What would it take for you to have the privilege of baptizing dozens of people this year? What if Eastview saw one-thousand people baptized into Christ this coming year alone? Why couldn't it happen? It can, but we have to follow the example of Tiharu and fearlessly make the gospel known at all times, in all situations, and in all opportunities. That's what it means to live a dangerous witness with an open mouth.

WEEK 5: THURSDAY;
A LOCAL PERSPECTIVE

OPEN MOUTH: MEET WAYNE STEWART

This week's theme might appear to elevate someone who talks incessantly. That would be a false conclusion and would certainly not describe Wayne Stewart. Wayne has been employed at State Farm, currently as a claim consultant, for the past twenty-seven years. Prior to that job, he briefly taught school in Arkansas City, Kansas. Rather than being a chronic talker, Wayne is a man who has trained himself to be an active listener and responder to the grace of God at work in his own life and in the routine circumstances of everyday life. He opens his mouth as God gives opportunity. He has been married to his wife, Sandy, since 1984. Allow me to introduce you to this father of two girls, Casey and Taylor, and a living example of God's reclaiming grace.

How did you become an apprentice to Jesus?

"I was a church kid who was saved at a young age while attending a Baptist youth camp, Lake Shetek, in Minnesota. It was a fire and brimstone night, and I had a deep conviction of my sin and a desire to say yes to Jesus. My grandfather was a fifth grade boys' Sunday school teacher, and I feared getting old enough to be in his class and not being saved. I couldn't see the rest of this Jesus-following life, especially the Lordship piece. There was no abuse in my home. I had no drug or alcohol problems. My mother and father have been married for over fifty years. My dad was frequently on the road, and, even when he was home, he was generally disconnected. My mom was and is a submissive angel who just wants to love and to be loved. I graduated from college with a good GPA, but something was missing. After our first daughter was born, Sandy and I began to experience a spiritual awakening. We lived in places like Garden City, Kansas, Wichita, Kansas, Broken Arrow, Oklahoma, and Kansas City, Kansas. Job promotions with State Farm kept us on the move, but, still, there was this spiritual hunger for more. Several churches provided some support, encouragement, and spiritual food, but, still, I wanted more. State Farm recognized my abilities almost immediately. I don't say that with any kind of pride or arrogance. I was promoted to my first management level position after just two and a half years. I loved the power of the jobs I held. I began to travel a great deal. I knew the dangers of being on the road but not firmly rooted in Christ, and I thought I could handle them on my own. I made a series of bad choices that strained our marriage to the breaking point and caused tremendous hurt to my daughters. We ended up moving to Bloomington in 2008."

What happened then?

"Jesus Christ brought me to my knees as I watched my wife and children suffer for almost two years because of what I was doing. I tried to blame Sandy, but when I finally held up a real mirror, the mirror of the truth of the Bible, the mirror of authentic manhood, I saw clearly who and what I was. I saw my heart wound. I finally confessed my sin and began the long journey back to being a man of integrity and faithfulness. Sandy forgave me. She has faithfully walked with me through all of this. I've come to recognize that no man is immune from the tricks of Satan. My passion in life is to serve the Lord by pouring God's truth through my life and testimony into other men. All men are vulnerable simply because we are men with wounded hearts. One of the qualities of an authentic man is to reject passivity, and that means to not allow compromise to enter our lives. All five senses must be totally surrendered to God on a 24-7 basis. If not, anyone of us may be one wrong decision away from starting down a path of sin."

You mentioned moving to Bloomington. How did you migrate here?

"We left Kansas City and a very rough church situation. As I mentioned earlier, we moved to Bloomington in 2008. We started attending Eastview immediately. We both wanted to get away from denominationalism and sensationalism. I began to get involved in a men's Bible study. It was in that study when God convicted me of my sin and rebellion. Sandy and I had contemplated divorce but sensed a calling from God to re-center our life. Words like healing, grace, and awakening are really true in my story. I still weep over my sinful decisions, but day by day God continues to put me back together. God has crafted me to speak to certain men. Jesus Christ delivered me, and I praise Him that it was not too late for me or for my family."

How is God using you at State Farm these days?

"I can give you an example. I was approached by one of my fellow workers, Tom Moss, who attends ECC. He told me that he wanted to live an authentic life and wondered if he and I could meet while we attended a claims leadership conference in Phoenix, Arizona. Originally, it was just going to be the two of us, but I suggested that we invite others guys to join us. A dozen or so of us met. What started as two morning gatherings has continued since we returned from Arizona, and we are regularly meeting for a Monday morning devotional and prayer time at work. More questions are being asked. God is opening doors. It is God's plan at work, not mine. I'm praying for opportunities to fearlessly speak for God. His grace is always sufficient."

WEEK 5: FRIDAY;
A PERSONAL PERSPECTIVE

If you've continued in your daily reading this week, you've had the chance to sit at the feet of Jesus as He taught about the Holy Spirit's power to speak in and through the believer in times of trials. You've journeyed with us to recount the incredible life and death of a faith-filled martyr who demonstrated the control and composure of a life yielded to the Spirit. Additionally, you've read inspiring testimonies of modern day men in India and Normal, IL. As we dive into another "personal perspective," let's review the accounts we've studied this week:

♦ A Biblical Perspective from Mark 13:9-11 (The Holy Spirit gives words to speak)

♦ An Historical Perspective of Perpetua (A noble woman martyred in 203 A.D.)

♦ A Cross-Cultural Perspective of Tiharu (church planter in India)

♦ A Local Perspective from Wayne Stewart (member at Eastview Christian Church)

If we are not careful, this theme of "Open Mouth" can leave us much like the typical spectators at a track meet. In the stadium, we're moved to cheer and to marvel at the effort and giftedness on display. We might even stand and scream with enthusiasm. Some might even remember the discipline and delight of running years ago, quietly reflecting on decades gone by. Yet, in our faith journey, there is always a personal call to climb out of the stands and to join the race!

What troubles me most about our "Open Mouth" opportunities is the tension between two truths. As we learned in Mark 13:9-11 (Monday's reading), the Holy Spirit will provide us with wisdom and words when challenges arise. In the moments when we are surprised by opportunities and fearful of inability, the Holy Spirit can overcome our inadequacies and demonstrate that He is able and providential. But does this ability mean that we should fail to prepare and plan? I'd like to suggest that Scripture champions our commitment to "open our mouths" in moments of preparation AND unpreparedness!

In chapter one of Joshua, we have an opportunity to listen in to God's "pep-talk" to Joshua. In these eighteen verses, God challenges Joshua to "be strong and courageous" four different times (vs. 6, 7, 9 and 18). In many ways, He is saying, "just take that first step ... open your mouth ... and I'll take it from there. I'm already at work here ... and I want to use you for My purposes." I would suggest that Joshua is exhorted to "be strong and courageous" because he was terrified and he needed the Holy nudge! When we think of this "Open Mouth" challenge, we might be experiencing similar emotions. There are times when we simply need to trust that God is already at work and will carry that work to completion.

On the other hand, you will find that God weaves in some other detail as He gives this "pep-talk" to Joshua. We read,

> **Be strong and very courageous**. Be careful to obey all the law my servant Moses gave you; do not turn from it to the right or to the left, that you may be successful wherever you go. *Do not let this Book of the Law depart from your mouth; meditate on it day and night, so that you may be careful to do everything written in it.* Then you will be prosperous and successful. **Do not be terrified; do not be discouraged, for the Lord your God will be with you wherever you go.** (Joshua 1:7-9, emphasis mine)

The sections in bold emphasize the challenge to overcome fear, backed with the promise that God would be with him. However, this is not a license to laziness or a lack of preparation. A closer look at the words in *italics* will help us to see that God had charged Joshua with carefully meditating on Scripture. This passage demonstrates the "twin truths" of our "Open Mouth" message. Wherever possible, we are to study the Word of God carefully so that we will better understand the ways of God and the will of God. Yet, in the moments that catch us off-guard, He has promised to give us the words to say. As in other areas of life, when we are weak, He will be strong!

This knowledge leaves us with a pressing question: "Will you courageously open your mouth to share about His ways even when you feel unprepared?" Take a moment to reflect on the times when you've ventured into a conversation about Jesus without all of the answers. Even more challenging, let's consider the times when we've stayed in the stands rather than participating on the field because we were not "strong and courageous." When we carefully listen, we'll hear God cheering us on to "get in the race" AND to continue to dwell in His Word so that we can "open our mouth" as God leads.

As you strive personally to apply the teaching of this week, act on at least one of the following:

♦ Journal about times when you've courageously "opened your mouth" to discuss the truths of God with someone in need.

♦ Discuss this week's reading with your small group, seeking the group's feedback and prayer support and for you further to develop the trust in Christ to speak on His behalf in various situations.

♦ Listen and look for the Spirit's leading in various settings. Then, begin to speak and to look for the Holy Spirit to give you words.

♦ Joshua 1:9 says, "Have I not commanded you? Be strong and courageous. Do not be terrified; do not be discouraged, for the Lord your God will be with you wherever you go." Meditate on this passage as it applies to your life.

WEEK 5: SATURDAY

On Saturdays throughout our study of "OPEN," we will pause to memorize one Scripture reference and to contemplate one thought-provoking question.

> Joshua 1:9 says, "Have I not commanded you? Be strong and courageous. Do not be terrified; do not be discouraged, for the Lord your God will be with you wherever you go." Memorize this verse today.

Often in times of testing and trials, I feel that I'm in the majority when I recognize that God is with me. Strength and courage to "open our mouths" comes like a flood when we consider His faithfulness and wisdom, available to us. Will you commit to speaking about God when the opportunity presents itself?

WEEK SIX
OPEN DOORS
"PRAYING FOR THE HOLY SPIRIT AT WORK"

MONDAY; A BIBLICAL PERSPECTIVE

"The only thing you need in order to sustain an effective approach to evangelism year after year after year is an ear fine-tuned to the promptings of the Holy Spirit" (Hybels, 2006, p. 35).

❖

Principle: Pray and follow the Spirit

❖

"Now, Lord, consider their threats and enable your servants to speak your word with great boldness...After they prayed, the place where they were meeting was shaken. And they were all filled with the Holy Spirit and spoke the word of God boldly"
(Acts 4:29, 31).

"Oh Lord," the prayer goes during the morning routine of getting dressed, "help me be a witness for you today." It is a sincere prayer and one the believer desires to live out. But somewhere between the first sip of coffee and the morning headlines, this godly focus shifts to the urgency of the day's schedule. On the drive to work, this good

Christian passes a broken-down car, reasoning that the lady inside had a cell phone and help was probably on the way.

During a quick stop for coffee, this disciple patiently waits for his latte while scanning his iPhone for emails. He overhears a couple talking about being new to town and wondering about finding a church but thinks it would be rude to interrupt a conversation uninvited. During a morning meeting, our Christ-follower notices that a colleague who is normally very upbeat is, instead, quiet and even sad. No time to talk though. The next meeting is in fifteen minutes.

Lunch with some non-believing co-workers presents an uneasy moment as everyone digs in without praying. A whisper of "thanks Lord" serves as a prayer for the meal and avoids any label of "Jesus Freak" that may have resulted from a longer prayer. The afternoon was a blur of e-mails, growth charts, and reading reports before braving the rush hour traffic. A quick stop at the grocers on the way home included a rather blunt question asked of our would-be evangelist: "Are you a Christian?" the checkout attendant asked out of nowhere. A faint "yes" was all he could manage and then a half-mumbled and awkward "have a nice day" as he grabbed the receipt.

The man in this story truly loves the Lord. And even though he is a little nervous, he really wants to be a witness for Him. He prayed for God to allow Him to talk of his faith, and the prayer was sincere.

But at the end of the day, the Spirit offered five opportunities to witness, and he hadn't spoken one word about Jesus. But why? Was God not interested in spreading His word on this particular day? Did his prayer go unanswered, and did the Spirit just not open up any doors? Or did this saint miss opportunities because he was not tuned into the Holy Spirit's wind of direction? I have to confess that this fictional caricature of a typical day is all too familiar to me. Maybe you recognize yourself here too. We need to change, but how? Simply put, evangelism requires prayer and following the Spirit. The two are inseparable!

Wherever the word of God is, the Spirit shows up. He was there hovering over the dark pre-creation mass of earth at the beginning when God actually spoke the words, "let there be light" (Genesis 1:3). He empowered the Old Testament prophets as they spoke and wrote the word of God on his behalf (II Peter 1:21). He came upon the Virgin Mary to create the living Word in her womb (Luke 1:35). He descended when the Word of God was baptized and began His ministry (Luke 3:22). He empowered the preached word of the early church by miraculously causing them to speak in many different languages (Acts 2:4). This same Spirit lives in us, leads us, and shows up every time we speak of the Living Word of God, Jesus! Therefore, if we are to speak for Him, we are going to need Holy Spirit power.

The early believers understood this need as described in Acts 4 and the verses we've noted above. In Acts 4:23, we find that Peter and John had just been released from prison, beating, and threats because they were preaching Jesus and causing a stir in Jerusalem. So, they called the believers together, and they had a prayer meeting. They prayed about how they were going to continue witnessing under threatening conditions. I propose that we follow their lead as we long to be dangerous witnesses of the gospel of Jesus Christ.

They prayed for God to enable them to speak His word with boldness. We have spent the last five weeks learning why we should share, what we should share, and how to share our faith with others, but, eventually, we actually have to do it. And here's the surprising truth: we can't do it on our own. Even the Apostles didn't dare speak on their own. They depended on the Holy Spirit to enable, to empower, and to give them boldness as they spoke. If we are to be bold witnesses for Jesus, we are going to have to pray more and more for the Holy Spirit to open doors and to make us bold.

These early believers not only prayed for boldness, but they spoke when and where the Holy Spirit moved. Admittedly, the scene at the end of this prayer time is pretty dramatic. The building actually shook, and the Holy Spirit poured into all of them the ability to speak the word of God in an obvious and powerful way. One might be inclined to say, "If the building shakes, I'll share my faith." But the Holy Spirit doesn't move exclusively in shaking buildings. He sometimes nudges. Often, He whispers. Jesus says He is like a breeze. The Holy Spirit convicts. He also encourages, gifts, and fills. Our problem in sharing our faith is not whether the Spirit is there or is interested; it is in our awareness of His presence.

If we are to become witnesses like those we see in the early church, if our neighbors, friends, co-workers, classmates, and family members have a chance of becoming Christ followers like us, and if we are to bring true revival to our city and our world, we are going to have to pray for more boldness, and we are going to have to start watching more closely for those opportunities the Spirit will inevitably provide. May we intensify our prayers for the message, and may we boldly speak when the Spirit does what He does. May we walk through hundreds of open doors!

WEEK 6: TUESDAY;
AN HISTORICAL PERSPECTIVE

DIETRICH BONHOEFFER
AN HISTORICAL PERSPECTIVE

Dietrich Bonhoeffer, one of the most remarkable Christians of the twentieth century, was born ten minutes ahead of his twin sister, Sabine, February 4, 1906. He entered a world in great flux. Political and social upheaval, along with World War 1, the Great Depression, the rise of Adolph Hitler to power, and the Second World War, would profoundly shape this disciple of Christ's life. Karl and Paula Bonhoeffer, Dietrich's parents, were highly educated, deeply loving, and genuinely caring for their family of eight children. Karl Bonhoeffer was an agnostic. He taught his children discipline in thought and speech. His primary and focusing lesson to this brood of eight was to speak only when you had something to say. Paula, in contrast, was a strong and faithful Lutheran Christian. She saw to it that the daily life of her family was filled with Bible reading and hymn singing. All in all, this was a well-adjusted and happy family where music was central. Dietrich even contemplated a career as a pianist. He could sight-read music at a very young age and played Mozart sonatas before he was ten. However, it was theology that captured his heart. From the age of thirteen onward, Dietrich did not waver in his desire to study theology and ultimately to pastor. The death of his brother, Walter, during World War 1 profoundly marked his life. His mother gave him Walter's Bible, and Dietrich used it the rest of his life for his daily devotions.

Bonhoeffer's university studies took him to Tubingen and Berlin. By the time he was twenty-one, he had earned his doctorate, graduating with the highest honors --summa cum laude. Some professors thought he was arrogant because of his independent thinking, but the truth rested more in the reality of his confidence in intellectual matters. After all, his father had shaped and molded him to be a certain kind of thinker. His theological studies required parish work, so Bonhoeffer began to teach a children's Sunday school class! He became so popular with the children that other classes wanted to join his. Eventually, Dietrich served a Lutheran congregation in Barcelona, Spain, as an assistant pastor. He preached, taught, pastored, and especially watched over the children's ministry. He loved his work with the little ones. He spent a year there working at communicating theology to apathetic businessmen, busy mothers, preoccupied teenagers, and adoring children. Amazing! It sounds like a fairy tale, except that back in Germany Adolph Hitler and the Nazis had risen to power. The Fuhrer had to be opposed. In spite of traveling abroad to America and England several times, Dietrich knew his place was back in Germany. He recognized that the evil of Hitler could not be defeated with cheap religion.

Bonhoeffer was torn. Should he go to India where he wanted to spend some time talking with Gandhi or return to Germany and take charge of a preacher's seminary? Jesus Christ and the Sermon on the Mount had taken hold of his life, and there was the unavoidable call to be salt and light in a decaying and darkened time. He knew something was wrong with the traditional church in Germany. Nationalism and Christianity had somehow been joined together in a sickening and compromising mix. There is so much to tell in this amazing story, but let us get to the heart of it. Dietrich had already begun to pray for the defeat of his own nation. He believed that it was the only way Germany could pay for all the suffering it had caused in the world. Eventually, he was obligated to stand up for the Jews and to stand against his own homeland.

Dietrich's involvement in the Valkyrie plot and in Operation 7 to assassinate Hitler and to smuggle Jews into neutral Switzerland ultimately and finally led to his arrest. On April 5, 1943, the Gestapo showed up at his door, and he spent time in several prisons, including the now-famous Cell 92, Tegel Prison, Buchenwald, and, finally, Flossenburg in Berlin. Twenty hours before his death, he led a small worship service where he prayed, read from Isaiah 53 and 1 Peter 1, and explained their meaning to his fellow prisoners. When he finished his prayer, two men in civilian clothes showed up, asked for him by name, and escorted him away. Those who witnessed this moment said he left bravely and spoke these final words to them: "This is the end. For me the beginning of life." The camp doctor at Flossenburg, years later, recorded these words in watching Bonhoeffer's final moments of life: "I saw Pastor Bonhoeffer, before taking off his prison garb, kneeling on the floor praying fervently to his God. I was most deeply moved by the way this lovable man prayed, so devout and so certain that God heard his prayer. At the place of execution, he again said a short prayer and then climbed the steps to the gallows, brave and composed. His death ensued after a few seconds. In the almost fifty years that I worked as a doctor, I have hardly ever seen a man die so entirely submissive to the will of God" (Metaxas, 2010, p. 532).

What will this next year hold for us? What will the decade ahead bring? Will we enter a new era of Christian martyrdom? Only God knows the answers to these questions. Our call and challenge is to pray that God's Spirit will be powerfully at work in and through us, His church. May He find us courageous to the end, as He did His servant Dietrich Bonhoeffer.

WEEK 6: WEDNESDAY;
A CROSS-CULTURAL PERSPECTIVE

THE TESTIMONY OF SARAT

Sarat was born into the Gada tribe in Central India. This tribe was quite large, numbering 600,000 people. Sarat's grandfather and father were both the leaders of the tribe. As the oldest son in the family, Sarat was positioned to lead the tribe one day. He was, in essence, a prince, a prince that would one day be broken, disowned, and then used to change his tribe forever.

To prepare Sarat for an honorable future and role in leading his tribe, his father sent him away to boarding school. Away from the influence of his family and tribe, Sarat began to fall into the wrong crowd. He would eventually find himself involved in drugs, alcohol, and the pursuits of this world. This path led him to selling marijuana to make quick money. It was on a drug run that Sarat was arrested with fifty pounds of marijuana in his vehicle. He was thrown in jail. He sat alone and confused for seven days before his father unexpectedly showed up and bailed him out. As he got in the car, he noticed his father was driving him home to his tribe. They rode in silence for seven hours. His father didn't say one word to him. As they pulled up to his home, Sarat noticed that all the tribal leaders and his family were at his house. As they got out of the truck, Sarat's father grabbed

his son's hand. He held it up in the air. He went on to list, in explic-
it detail, all the sins of his son and the shame he had brought on himself, his family, and the tribe. Then, in a moment Sarat will never forget, he looked Sarat in the eyes and publicly disowned him in front
of the tribe: "I have no son."

As one can only imagine, this experience humiliated and wounded Sarat in ways that words cannot describe. Despised and rejected
by his own family and tribe, he returned to the town in which he was
arrested. He made plans to kill himself; he had nothing to live for.
One night, he found himself in the local market buying a highly con-
centrated and potent insecticide. He knew that, if he drank the entire
bottle, it would be powerful enough to kill him. His plan was to drink
it that very evening to end his pain. As he walked through the town
square with the bag in his hand, he heard a crowd gathering around a
man who was talking quite loud with great passion. Sarat found himself navigating towards the voice only to find it was a preacher sharing the good news of Jesus Christ.

The preacher caught Sarat's eye and recognized him as the oldest
son of the Gada tribal leader. Miles from home, on the verge of trying to end his own life, he was known by someone. This encounter
could only be orchestrated by the Holy Spirit. The preacher saw how
distraught Sarat looked and stopped to talk with him. He took him

home for three days and loved him like his own son. They ate togeth-er, cried together, and prayed together, and Sarat ended up meeting his Lord and Savior that weekend. Sarat became the first person in the entire Gada tribe to follow Jesus.

Although Sarat had nowhere to go and nowhere to turn, God providentially connected Sarat with CICM's biblical academy. Sarat wanted to learn more about the God that waited for him, a true prodi-gal son to come home. The God that saw Sarat spiritually ran to him, threw his arms around him, and welcomed home His son. Sarat grew in the wisdom and knowledge of God, and, upon graduation, was commissioned to go back to his tribe. At graduation, he said, "I don't know what to preach, but I do know Jesus, and he has changed me. I'll show my people my changed life as a testimony." Sarat prayed that the Holy Spirit would open doors to share Jesus with his people. He prayed for his parents as well who, at the time, he had been estranged from for over five years.

When he arrived back at his tribe, people were astonished at his transformation. As he began to share his testimony and to preach the gospel, people began to respond to this prodigal son. Not hundreds, but thousands of Gada people came to know the Lord within a few years. And then, Sarat got the call that still brings tears to his eyes. Sarat's father wanted to meet with him, and he wanted to meet the man that had changed his son. Sarat asked Aai Lall, founder of CICM, to accompany him home to the place of his public disownment. They prayed that God, through his Holy Spirit, would do something miraculous. It was a tense drive for Sarat, filled with pain, regret, and a simple trust that God was in control.

Over the course of three days, Sarat and Ajai talked with his parents about the incredible love of Jesus. People were praying. The Spirit was moving. After three days, Sarat was reconciled to his family and baptized his father into Christ. Their relationship was restored, and Sarat was reinstated as his son. Tears were shed, and wounds began to heal. Above all, this prodigal son experienced reconciliation with his heavenly father and, now, his earthly father. The Holy Spirit continues to move in the Gada tribe today. Sarat has led over six-thousand Gada tribesmen to the Lord, and there are several CICM church planters working among the tribe today because of Sarat's influence.

This is the story of a prodigal prince coming home, but behind it is the story the Holy Spirit was weaving together. The life of a dangerous witness is Spirit-led and empowered. Sarat boldly went back to his people, but only because he was praying for open doors. A dangerous witness can't walk through doors without first praying them open. When we begin to see the passions of this world dwarfed by our prayers for the lost, we will also see revival. We'll see the Holy Spirit open doors, and then the only question left for us is whether we're willing to walk through them. Are you praying?

WEEK 6: THURSDAY;
A LOCAL PERSPECTIVE

OPEN DOORS: MEET CONNIE UROSEVICH

I like meeting people with some life experience. It's not that I in any way devalue those who are younger than I am. They have much to share with me and teach me as well, but there is something about encountering people who have lived a while and have been knocked around a bit that especially blesses me. Connie Urosevich is just such a person.

Connie, how did you become a Jesus-follower?

"I was raised in a very large Presbyterian Church, in Omaha, Nebraska. The Gospel was preached there. I sang in the choir and was a regular church-goer, but somehow I managed never to make a personal commitment to Christ. I was married in 1969 and tried to live as a Christian, but Christ was not the center of my life. We had moved to Rockford, Illinois, and as we began to raise our children, I saw the need to attend church. Providentially, we lived next door to a Christian couple, and I began to attend a Bible study with the wife of that couple. I felt a longing inside of me, but I didn't know what it was. As our children grew up, my son began to date a girl from another Christian family. There was something unique about that young lady, and I even said to myself, 'I wonder what makes her dif-

ferent than me?' In 1990, my husband asked for a divorce. I was devastated. It was the first time that I saw myself as a sinner in need of
a Savior."

What happened then?

"Initially, my family was torn apart. Eventually, God restored my
relationship with my children. Often, children are leveraged between
parents. I didn't want to be the kind of woman who was constantly
critical of her former spouse. My son was now a freshman in college,
and my daughter was a freshman in high school. She went through a
deep-seated rebellion of ten years. I prayed persistently for her. It was
a very painful decade. She is now married, has three children of her
own, and is a faithful Christ-follower. In May, 1990, I was attending
a Bible study that led me to read the Scriptures for the very first time
on my own. I began to practice a daily quiet time. I also begin to pray
regularly and often. In 1991, my daughter and I moved to Pontiac and
attended church again."

Was there a defining moment in all of this transition time?

"It was a strange time when God took all my history of being in
church, knowing some Bible things, seeing a Christian counselor,
and He began to awaken me to Himself. While seeing that counselor,
I was told for the first time in my life, 'You are passive-aggressive.'
I heard it as sin. I was shocked. I could hardly imagine this could be

true of me, yet it was. I meditated deeply on that day and that experience. What had I done to facilitate my divorce? I got to the place where I asked Jesus to come into my life, and He did. I eventually began to look for work. I found a job at an accounting firm in Bloomington, but I had no accounting background and had never taken a college course. The company was willing to pay for some accounting courses, and so, at age forty-five, I took two courses at Lincoln College. My daughter had left home, and I needed to get closer to work, so I moved to Bloomington in 1993."

Where did that educational journey take you?

"After those first two classes at Lincoln College, I ended up earning a BS degree in accounting at ISU and eventually completed an MS degree there in 1998. God provided the resources. He was so faithful. I retired the first time in 2011, but I've continued working part-time as an accountant assistant. I battled breast cancer in 2001, but it was found early enough that, with radiation treatments, God has given me a second chance on life. He has taught me so much, especially about my dependency upon Him. My first reaction about most things these days is to pray first. That hasn't always been true of me."

How did you end up at ECC?

"The second Sunday I was in Bloomington, I visited ECC, and I met two people I knew, and I felt like I had come home. I was attending Saturday evening services back then, studying for the CPA, and that time of worship was perfect for me. I began ushering, and, ultimately, twenty years later, that role has led me to serving in the food pantry and being a small group leader."

How does your story connect with this week's theme? Do you think of yourself as an evangelist?

"I think about all those people who prayed for me--aunts, grandmother, mom, and so many others. One of my aunts told me that my grandmother prayed for me before I was born. I am so thankful and immensely blessed by my spiritual legacy. Now I am a grandmother praying for my grandchildren. I also think about those I could be praying for in my neighborhood, those at my work place, and people I simply meet here and there. I journal daily, still memorize Scripture, read my Bible, practice some of the disciplines like fasting and personal retreating. Susie Baker and I enjoyed a retreat together at the Chiara Center in Springfield not long ago. Truthfully, I don't think of myself as an evangelist. I want my life to be an expression of the Gospel for others. I have a regular prayer practice where I pray for those who are ill, my small group, those serving overseas, my family, for those in leadership at ECC, and those who don't know Jesus. I really do pray for the Holy Spirit to be at work."

WEEK 6: FRIDAY;
A PERSONAL PERSPECTIVE?

In this sixth and final week of our study, we've continued the pattern set in week one, giving us multiple perspectives from various times and places. Before we dive into some personal application for this week, let's take inventory of the perspectives we've covered in the past few days:

♦ A Biblical Perspective from Acts 4:23-31 (The Holy Spirit opens doors)

♦ An Historical Perspective of Dietrich Bonhoeffer (A twentieth century pastor/prisoner)

♦ A Cross-Cultural Perspective of Sarat (church planter/prince in India)

♦ A Local Perspective from Connie Urosevich (member at Eastview Christian Church)

The more I read of Christians in other eras and places, the more I appreciate the grandeur of our God. His story is truly breathtaking. His creativity in reaching each of us in unique ways continues to bless and inspire me. How is He continuing to open doors, that we might play a small part in the great saga of our King's rescue story?

The book of Acts is filled with awe-inspiring stories. Within the pages of this book, we find stories of heroism, travel, conversions, and miracles. We also find thirty-two speeches that weave elements of story throughout powerful testimonies. In the midst of these riveting speeches and stories, there is a compelling undercurrent of the Holy Spirit's activity as foreman and forerunner for the "works of the Apostles."

In chapter 14, we read of Paul and Barnabas as they travelled to various cities to establish and to encourage the churches. Upon return to Antioch, "they gathered the church together and reported all that God had done through them and how he had opened the door of faith to the Gentiles" (vs. 27). Did you catch that? Paul and Barnabas had been on the front-lines of the miraculous. They had even been mistaken for gods (vs. 12-13), and the people sought to offer sacrifices to them! Yet, Paul and Barnabas knew there was only One who had "opened the doors." They gathered the people to "report all that God had done ... and how he had opened the door of faith." On a very practical level, Paul and Barnabas had to *recognize* open doors, to *respond* to open doors personally, and to *report* open doors to others.

Truthfully, the idea of waiting for "open doors" is challenging to different people in different ways. Depending on your temperament, waiting might be something you circumvent with your own self-agenda or an excuse for inactivity and passivity! In his book *Spiritual Influence*, Mel Lawrenz observes,

> The passive approach is: wait to see what comes your way. The aggressive approach is: make your own way. There is another possibility: obediently follow God's way. If the

temptation of the bullish influencer is to knock down one wall after another, the temptation of more passive people is to dawdle and procrastinate in the name of waiting for the Spirit of God. Following God's way is not the leisurely way; it is harder work than the bullish way. (89)

We know that God "opens doors," but the most pressing question for many of us has been, "How do I know whether this is a God-ordained opportunity or a distraction from His direction for my life?" Uncertainty in this area will cause some to be "bullish influencers" while others will passively procrastinate. While this topic is profoundly difficult to address, there may be some helpful principles for you to consider as you walk in obedience and help others to do the same. Consider the following questions (adapted from *Spiritual Influence* by Mel Lawrenz):

♦ *Is the opportunity consistent with your sense of calling?*

♦ We need to constantly examine our "yes" and protect our "yes" by courageously saying "no" to good opportunities that are not God opportunities.

♦ There is a difference between "weights" and "sin" (see Heb. 12:1). Weights are the subtle things (not necessarily "sin things") that hinder us from running the race set before us.

♦ *Is this opportunity God's way of redirecting your calling, purposes, or objectives?*

♦ In times of major decision-making, we need to be familiar with His voice as He leads.

♦ Are we willing to "die" to our agenda routinely, freeing us to "live" for His agenda?

♦ *Does this opportunity align with biblical values?*

♦ God does not seek to accomplish His will in contrast to His Word!

♦ Do trusted people affirm the alignment between this opportunity and biblical teaching?

♦ *If the opportunity requires the movement of others, is God moving them as well?*

♦ God's sovereignty is on display as He orchestrates many stories to harmonize with His story.

♦ God often authenticates His agenda by the confirmation of multiple witnesses.

Are you "open" to the Holy Spirit's lead? Do you recognize "open doors"? While the questions above are intended to guide us in our decision making, let's not forget the overall thrust of this study. We're talking about "open doors" that are opportunities to share Christ with others. Imagine a life of obedience and awareness to the Spirit's leading. Imagine a church where thousands of people pray for "open doors" and then boldly enter to share the hope of Christ!

As you strive to apply the teaching of this week personally, act on at least one of the following:

♦ Regarding Acts 14, we noted that there are three practical applications. We need to *recognize, respond* and *report.* Which of these do you most readily accomplish? Why?

♦ Discuss this week's reading with your small group, seeking the group's feedback and prayer support for you further to develop the ability to discern the "open doors" around you.

♦ What doors are you currently forcing open by your own might or will?

♦ What doors are you hesitant to enter, even though they appear to have been opened for you?

♦ Colossians 4:3-4 says, "And pray for us, too, that God may open a door for our message, so that we may proclaim the mystery of Christ, for which I am in chains. Pray that I may proclaim it clearly as I should." Meditate on this passage as it applies to your life.

WEEK 6: SATURDAY

On Saturdays throughout our study of "OPEN," we will pause to

memorize one Scripture reference and to contemplate one thought-

provoking question.

> Colossians 4:3-4 says, "And pray for us, too, that God may
> open a door for our message, so that we may proclaim the
> mystery of Christ, for which I am in chains. Pray that I may
> proclaim it clearly, as I should." Memorize this verse
> today.

This passage clearly demonstrates the dance between the Holy

Spirit's work and our willingness to cooperate. Twice in this passage,

Paul pleads for prayer (knowing the power is His, not ours). Yet, Paul

does not retreat from responsibility in proclaiming "clearly," even if

"in chains." Are you prayerfully seeking "open doors" to share the

Gospel?

OPEN
Study Guide

Week 1: OPEN LIVES
Week 2: OPEN ARMS
Week 3: OPEN WITNESS
Week 4: OPEN TO ALL
Week 5: OPEN MOUTH
Week 6: OPEN DOORS

INTRODUCTION

Thank you for your willingness to participate in this study! Our hope and prayer is that this material will work its way into the lives of thousands of Christ-followers, that we will remain "open" to God's work in us, and that our lives would be "open" to the lost people of our community.

As our groups journey together through these six sessions, we are confident that God will transform our hearts to mirror His own. Additionally, we pray that many would be drawn to the salvation that only Jesus can offer through the "dangerous witness" of the church.

In order to get the most out of this study, please commit to the daily reading in this book and review each week's study prior to meeting as a group. Your thoughtful participation will challenge and inspire others.

In Christ,
Jim Probst
Pastor of Small Groups
Eastview Christian Church
www.eastviewchurch.net

"OPEN LIVES"

DISCUSSION STARTERS: (SELECT ONE)

1. If this is a newly-formed group, have everyone introduce themselves. Briefly describe the hobby you would incorporate into your life if you had the time and resources for it.

2. If this is a pre-existing group, have members finish one of the following sentences:

- I'm most hopeful that this new study will ...
- I'm most fearful that this new study will ...
- This group has been most rewarding to me when ...
- When I think about sharing my faith, I ...

KEY WORD STUDY:

Shuwb: This Hebrew word communicates a vivid word picture in the Old Testament that is translated as "repent," "turn back," or "return." In Hosea 3:5, we see a parallel between Gomer's unfaithfulness and that of Israel. In either case, rebellion is met with a call to "return."

KEY SCRIPTURE:

"But in your hearts set apart Christ as Lord. Always be prepared to give an answer to everyone who asks you to give the reason for the hope that you have. But do this with gentleness and respect" (1 Peter 3:15).

SOUND BITES (FROM THE VIDEO TEACHING):

- "Hosea literally becomes a living testimony of God's redemptive power." –Mike Baker
- "You can't just tell people the right way. You have to pursue the right way." –Mike Baker
- "What does your life say about God in your life?"? –Mike Baker

- "How do you call someone to "shuwb" without being offensive? –J.K. Jones

DISCUSSION:

1. Select one of the "Discussion Starters" above, and share your response with one another.?

2. Have someone begin this study by leading the group in prayer.

3. Introduce the "group covenant" to all of the group members and discuss some basic expectations for the group (download this resource at www.eastviewchurch.net/smallgroups).

4. Briefly share the big idea of this six-week study entitled "OPEN" (see the introduction and leader's guide in the book for more insight).

5. Our daily reading for this week (and the following weeks) will consist of various "perspectives" that express our theme. Biblical, historical, cross-cultural, local, and personal perspectives will give us varied examples to expand our understanding for each week's theme. Which of these perspectives have you/will you find most inspirational? Explain.

6. Watch the video segment for week one, entitled "Open Lives – Your First and Best Witness is the Life You Live."

7. Take a moment to read/review the "sound bites" in this session. What was the most insightful or impactful comment you read or heard on this subject?

8. As a group, read 1 Peter 3:15. How does this passage coincide with the message of Hosea that we just watched in our video teaching?

9. Read the following passages and discuss the importance of integrity in our Christian witness (Psalm 119:80; Proverbs 2:7-8; 2 Corinthians 1:12; Titus 2:7-8).

10. Take a moment to reflect on the past year of your life. Have there been times that you've been asked to give "a reason for the hope that you have"? What does this reveal about the "openness" of your life?

11. Toward the end of the video teaching, J.K. Jones commented on Mike Baker's teaching by simply saying, "Not perfect lives … forgiven lives." How do you navigate the tightrope of living a life of integrity AND trusting in His grace when you fall short?

12. What questions about "Open Lives" remain unanswered at this time? How can the group help?

13. Pray together as a group with an emphasis on living "Open Lives."

BETWEEN THE MEETINGS:

1) Take time to reflect on the delicate balance of living "open lives" of integrity and grace. What do others see in you?

2) Continue in your daily reading of "OPEN."

3) Memorize and meditate on 1 Peter 3:15 (see Saturday's daily reading).

4) Pray that the members of your group grow closer to Christ and one another through this study.

"OPEN ARMS"

DISCUSSION STARTERS: (SELECT ONE)

1. Who is your favorite teacher from school years? What made that teacher so effective for you? What does that choice say about your learning style?

2. What is your favorite restaurant in town? When was the last time you ate there?

KEY QUOTE:

"I want to eat less often with saints and more often with sinners. I want some of my best friends to be lost – but not for long" (Chambers, 2009, p. 14).

KEY SCRIPTURE:

"Jesus answered them, 'It is not the healthy who need a doctor, but the sick. I have not come to call the righteous, but sinners to repentance'" (Luke 5:32).

SOUND BITES:

- "In a moment of honest, unfiltered, soul-searching transparency, ask yourself the following three questions:
- What am I willing to do to connect with people who don't know Jesus?
- How much am I really willing to sacrifice?

- What's the unspoken limit in my mind and heart as to what I'll sacrifice to share the ridiculous love of Jesus with people who are eternally lost"? (Tyler Hari, *OPEN*).
- "I'd like to suggest that the 'us' and 'them' language is not 'us vs. them,' but 'us for them.' The use of these pronouns is not meant to be divisive, but distinctive ... we have a message and ministry of reconciliation" (Jim Probst, *OPEN*).
- Referencing John Stott, J.K. Jones notes, "The living God is a missionary God."
- "How have you attempted to go to your own Nineveh?" (J.K. Jones).

DISCUSSION:

1. Select one of the "Discussion Starters" above, and share your response with one another.?

2. Have someone begin this study by leading the group in prayer.

3. Invite someone to give a 60 second review of last week's main theme (Open Lives).

4. Briefly share the big idea of this six-week study, entitled "OPEN" (see the introduction and leader's guide in the book for more insight).

5. Share one highlight from your daily reading of *OPEN* this week.

6. Watch the video segment for week two, entitled "Open Arms."

7. Take a moment to read/review the "sound bites" in this session. We've read or heard examples from Jesus, Polycarp, Sanjay, Mark Hapke, the Apostle Paul, and Jonah. Which has left the most vivid impression on you regarding this topic?

8. As a group, read Luke 5:27-32 and 1 Thessalonians 2:7-8. How do these passages coincide with the message of Jonah that we just watched in our video teaching?

9. Read Jonah 4:1-11. This segment of Scripture could be labeled "God's Great Compassion." How has this compassion been extended to/by you? (This would be a great time for the group leader to share the story of God's redemption in his/her own life).

10. Re-read the first sound bite in this week's study. Share your answer to at least one of these questions:

11. Who comes to mind as you consider your own response to this teaching on "Open Arms?"

12. How can the group help you?

13. Pray together as a group with an emphasis on demonstrating "Open Arms."

BETWEEN THE MEETINGS:

1) Take time to reflect on the people that God has placed in your circle of influence. Who might need to hear a message of repentance and reconciliation? How might God use you to share that message with them?

2) Continue in your daily reading of "OPEN."

3) Memorize and meditate on 1 Thessalonians 2:8 (see Saturday's daily reading).

4) Pray that the members of your group may be able to share their testimonies with others throughout this study.

"OPEN WITNESS"

DISCUSSION STARTERS: (SELECT ONE)

1. Who is the greatest story teller you have personally known? What did you like about his/her story telling style?

2. What genre of movie do you prefer to watch (action, comedy, drama, horror, etc.)? Why?

KEY WORD STUDY:

"Natsal" is the Hebrew word meaning to snatch away, to deliver, to rescue or save. This word occurs 213 times in the Old Testament and summarizes the plea of Rahab in Joshua 2:13. Additionally, this word highlights God's work among His people throughout the Bible.

KEY SCRIPTURE:

John 5:24 says, "I tell you the truth, whoever hears my word and believes him who sent me has eternal life and will not be condemned; he has crossed over from death to life."

SOUND BITES:

- "Every story (rescue story) begins with us saying that God is who He said He is" (Mike Baker).
- In the video teaching, J.K. Jones comments, "What does the Rahab story tell us about God? Nobody is outside of God's reach. With God, there is always the chance for a turn-around story."

- Paraphrasing Bill Hybels, Mike Baker noted 5 tips to sharing your own rescue story.
  - Be brief
  - Be clear
  - Be simple
  - Be humble
  - Be yourself
- "You have a story. A story that can shape people, transform lives, and change history. And God, in His tender mercy, stewards us thousands of opportunities to share that story" (Tyler Hari).
- In this week's daily reading, Jim Probst says, "Looking closely at Acts 26:1-29, we see some significant points that may be transferable in sharing our own stories:
- Paul's testimony is conveyed in three phases:
  - First, Paul speaks of his life prior to becoming a Christian (Acts 26:1-11).
  - Second, Paul shares a detailed account of his conversion experience (Acts 26:12-18).
  - Third, Paul demonstrates the kind of change that has resulted from his commitment to Christ (Acts 26:19-29).
- Paul's testimony is specific and focused.
- Paul's testimony provokes a response (see vs. 28-29).
- Paul's testimony glorifies God, not a sinful past.
- Paul's testimony demonstrates new life in Christ."

DISCUSSION:

1. Select one of the "Discussion Starters" above, and share your response with one another.?
2. Have someone begin this study by leading the group in prayer.
3. Invite someone to give a 60 second review of last week's main theme ("Open Arms").
4. Share one highlight from your daily reading of *OPEN* this week.
5. Watch the video segment for week three, entitled "Open Witness."

6. Take a moment to read/review the "sound bites" in this session.

7. We've read or heard examples from Jesus, Justin Martyr, Pastor Benyu, John Ashenfelter, the Apostle Paul, and Rahab. Which example has left the most vivid impression on you regarding this topic?

8. John Ashenfelter said, "God pursues us and He invites us into that pursuit." In what ways is God pursuing you or preparing you in this season of life?

9. As a group, read Acts 26:1-29. Is there anything we can learn from Paul as we prepare to communicate our own story?

10. Get into groups of 2-3 and share your own story of "natsal" or rescue. Consider the principles highlighted in the "sound bites." Briefly share your story (3 minutes).

11. What is your greatest concern in sharing your testimony with those who are apart from Christ?

12. Pray together as a group, asking the Lord to give you opportunities to share your story in the coming week.

BETWEEN THE MEETINGS:

1) Write out your testimony, reflecting on His saving grace and your opportunities to share with others.

2) Continue in your daily reading of "OPEN."

3) Memorize and meditate on John 5:24 (see Saturday's daily reading).

4) Pray that the members of your group may be able to share their testimonies this week.

5) Prepare to share THE story in the coming week.

"OPEN TO ALL"

DISCUSSION STARTERS: (SELECT ONE)

1. Imagine that you are in an elevator and someone asks about the Eastview vision t-shirt you are wearing. What is your 30 second response?

2. If you could trade places with another person (historical, current, or fictional) for one day, which person would you choose and why?

KEY WORD STUDY:

Regarding 1 Corinthians 15:3-4, Mike Baker notes, "Paul uses the Greek word *protos* to describe the faith statement he was passing on. We translate the Greek into 'first importance' because this word means 'that which comes first' (as in the first thing in a sequence), but it also means 'first in priority.' In other words, according to the Bible, the death, burial, and resurrection of Jesus are the most important truths we have to believe and to share about our faith."

KEY SCRIPTURE:

John 3:16-17 says, "For God so loved the world that he gave his one and only Son, that whoever believes in him shall not perish but have eternal life. For God did not send his Son into the world to condemn the world, but to save the world through him."

SOUND BITES:

- "If you are a Christ follower, then you are called, equipped, and expected to share the gospel. No exceptions!" (Hybels, 2006, p. 61).

- Romans 1:16 declares, "I am not ashamed of the gospel, because it is the power of God for the salvation of everyone who believes; first for the Jew, then for the Gentile."
- 2 Peter 3:9 reads, "The Lord is not slow in keeping his promise, as some understand slowness. He is patient with you, not wanting anyone to perish, but everyone to come to repentance."
- Referencing 2 Peter 3:9, J.K. Jones referred to the Father as "This all-inclusive God," while Mike Baker added, "It is the most inclusive club in the world."
- "…we need more than a clever t-shirt or an affiliation with a church. As Christ followers, we are expected to know and to share, not just our story, but how it intersects with THE story. The Great Commission was not intended only for a small band of first century disciples – it was intended for me, for you, and for all who will call on the name of Jesus as Lord and Savior" (Jim Probst).

DISCUSSION:

1. Select one of the "Discussion Starters" above, and share your response with one another.?

2. Have someone begin this study by leading the group in prayer.

3. Invite a member to share a testimony with the whole group.

4. Share one highlight from your daily reading of *OPEN* this week.

5. As a group, compare and contrast the content of 1 Corinthians 15:3-4 with that of Acts 26:23. In both cases, Paul communicates about the most significant concepts of our faith. Read and remark on both passages.

6. Take a moment to read/review the "sound bites" in this session.

7. Watch the video segment for week four, entitled "Open To All."

8. What part of this video teaching was most helpful for you?

9. Pass out two napkins to each group member. On one napkin, sketch out "THE story" as demonstrated in this video teaching. Save the other napkin for use as you practice this method between the meetings.

10. Get into groups of 2-3 and share THE story to the best of your ability. Look for more resources and insights at www.eastview-church.net/smallgroups. Consider the principles highlighted in the "sound bites." Briefly share THE story (3 minutes).

11. Statistics vary from study to study, but one thing is overwhelmingly clear. The vast majority of professing Christians neglect to share their hope in Christ with others. In your opinion, why is there such a gap between personal belief and personal evangelism?

12. Pray together as a group, asking the Lord to give you opportunities to share THE story in the coming week.

BETWEEN THE MEETINGS:

1) Write out THE story on one of your napkins this week, reflecting on the things of "first importance" and your opportunities to share with others.

2) Continue in your daily reading of "OPEN."

3) Memorize and meditate on John 3:16-17 (see Saturday's daily reading).

4) Pray that the members of your group may be able to share their testimonies within the context of THE story this week.

5) Share the Gospel with a friend, family member, or co-worker this week.

KNOWING & SHARING
THE GREATEST STORY EVER TOLD:

CREATION:

The story begins with *God*. God spoke and *created* everything – the pinnacle was a garden of paradise called Eden. His masterpiece was Adam and Eve, who reflected God's image. They were created with the purpose of worshipping, loving, serving, and enjoying relationship with God. There was perfect *harmony* in the beginning, exactly the way God intended. No pain, suffering, sickness or death were present. There was complete love, acceptance, and intimacy between God and man, Adam and Eve, and throughout creation.

FALL:

God gave Adam and Eve freedom to make decisions and to govern the earth with one rule: not to eat fruit from a specific tree. One day, God's enemy, a fallen angel named Satan, came in the form of a serpent and lied to Adam and Eve. He deceived them into thinking God wasn't good and didn't have their best interests in mind. As a result, they knowingly *disobeyed* God. In rebellion, Adam and Eve ate the fruit. Like a virus, sin entered all of creation and the hearts of Adam and Eve. Sin, suffering, and pain were passed down from generation to generation; all of creation was distorted from its original design. All of the bad and evil in this world are a result of sin. We are all guilty. All of us have sinned and fallen short, and the *consequence* is not only death, but eternal separation from a loving God. We *need* to be rescued.

RESCUE:

God removed Adam and Eve from Eden as a result of their sin but He left them with a promise of rescue and hope. He *promised* to send someone to save them from sin and death. Over the next centuries, God prepared the way for this person who would become the Savior of the world. Exact details of His birth, life, and death were recorded in the Bible. In fact, the whole Bible ultimately points to this one person as the focal point of all human history. Who was he? Simply, He was God. God became human in the person of Jesus Christ almost 2,000 years ago, fulfilling all predictions in the Old Testament. His birth was miraculous, and his life was perfect. He willingly, obediently, and sufficiently died on a cross to pay for the sins of mankind, according to God's plan. In the greatest display of mercy and grace the world has ever known, Jesus' life and death became a substitute for all who would trust in Him. The grave couldn't hold Jesus. He rose from the dead, fulfilling His earthly mission to defeat sin by dying on the cross and defeating death by rising from the dead – just as God *promised*. Forty days later, he returned to Heaven where He reigns as the rightful king.

RESTORATION:

For all of those who trust in Jesus, God has promised He will make *all things new*. The new heaven and new earth will be completely free of sin and selfishness – a place of perfect friendship with God, others, and all creation. Lives will no longer be plagued by pain, broken hearts, sickness, or death. Everything will be restored to the way it was meant to be. The new earth will once again be the perfect home God intended for His creation. The most wonderful part is that we will be *with God forever*, experiencing complete joy. The Gospel is saving us *from* (eternal separation from God) and saving us *unto* (abundant life, both now and eternally). Simply put, Jesus rescues us to eternal life and for everyday life.

WEEK FIVE

"OPEN MOUTH"

KEY WORD STUDY:

Tame' is the Hebrew word uttered by the prophet Isaiah when he encountered God in Isaiah 6:5. This word is translated as "unclean" in the English and can be defined as "polluted" or "defiled" as well. It is interesting to note that this is the same word lepers were to shout as they came near those without the disease!

KEY SCRIPTURE:

Mark 13:11 reads, "Whenever you are arrested and brought to trial, do not worry beforehand about what to say. Just say whatever is given you at the time, for it is not you speaking, but the Holy Spirit."

SOUND BITES:

- In Monday's daily reading, Mike Baker notes, "Christians often get so worried, anticipating the sequence of potential questions, conversational turns, and faith roadblocks that will jeopardize their witnessing opportunities. We should realize 'it is not you speaking, but the Holy Spirit.'"

- "Begin with your testimony of what Jesus has done for you, share the good news of His saving love and grace, and boldly proclaim it as a representative of God. You'll be surprised by what the Spirit says through you!" (Mike Baker).
- J.K. Jones succinctly notes in the video teaching, "God wins when we witness."
- In this week's reading, Tyler Hari notes, "We might be tempted to shy away from Tiharu's story. Instead of inspiring us, it could cause some of us to say, 'God could never use me in that way,' as we dismiss the possibility. But let's not be so quick to limit what God could do through the life of just one dangerous witness. God can use us, right here in Bloomington-Normal, to do the miraculous if we'll let Him."
- In reference to Joshua 1:7-9, Jim Probst notes, "This passage demonstrates the 'twin truths' of our 'Open Mouth' message. Wherever possible, we are to study the Word of God carefully so that we will better understand the ways of God and the will of God. Yet, in the moments that catch us off guard, He has promised to give us the words to say."

DISCUSSION:

1. Select one of the "Discussion Starters" above, and share your response with one another.?
2. Have someone begin this study by leading the group in prayer.
3. Invite a member of the group to share the gospel with the whole group. Hearing another example of THE story will help others to sharpen their own abilities to communicate this truth … and it will gently stretch the volunteer!
4. Ask a group member to read Wednesday's daily reading about Tiharu in its entirety. It is a captivating story of courage and God's providential work!
5. Take a moment to read/review the first three "sound bites" in this session.

6. Read Isaiah 6:1-8. Notice the completely different responses from Isaiah in verses 5 and 8. How do you think you would have responded in this situation?

7. Watch the video segment for week five, entitled "Open Mouth."

8. What part of this video teaching was most helpful for you?

9. Can you relate to the kind of rejection that Isaiah faced? How would you handle such a consistent rejection? What would be required to overcome such rejection?

10. Read Joshua 1:7-9 and the fifth "sound bite" from this study. Do you tend to trust more in your preparation or in the Holy Spirit's provision? Explain.

11. Pray together as a group, asking the Lord to give you courage as you "open your mouth" this week. Additionally, look for opportunities to invite someone to a church service, the small group, or a one-to-one discussion where they can hear the Gospel this week.

BETWEEN THE MEETINGS:

1) Prayerfully invite someone in your circle of influence to experience fellowship with the Father through a relationship with the Son.

2) Continue in your daily reading of "OPEN."

3) Memorize and meditate on Joshua 1:9 (see Saturday's daily reading).

4) Begin to discuss the next steps in your small group. What will you study next? How will you demonstrate a "dangerous witness" individually and as a group?

5) Contact a group member to follow up on the prayer requests you've shared this week

"OPEN DOORS"

KEY WORD STUDY:

Ruwach is the Hebrew word translated as "breath," "wind," or "spirit" in English. In 2 Kings 2:9, Elisha requests a "double portion" of Elijah's spirit upon his departure. Just as Elisha recognized the need for the work of the spirit in his ministry, we recognize the need for the Spirit to empower and guide us.

KEY SCRIPTURE:

Colossians 4:3-4 reads, "And pray for us, too, that God may open a door for our message, so that we may proclaim the mystery of Christ, for which I am in chains. Pray that I may proclaim it clearly, as I should."

SOUND BITES:

- "We have spent the last five weeks learning why we should share, what we should share, and how to share our faith with others, but, eventually we have to do it. And here's the surprising truth: we can't do it on our own. Even the Apostles didn't dare speak on their own. They depended on the Holy Spirit to enable, to empower, and to give them boldness as they spoke. If we are to be bold witnesses for Jesus, we are going to have to pray more and more for the Holy Spirit to open doors and to make us bold" (Mike Baker).

- "How can we cultivate an Elisha-like awareness of the Holy Spirit's work?" (J.K. Jones).

- "The passive approach is: wait to see what comes your way. The aggressive approach is: make your own way. There is another possibility: obediently follow God's way. If the temptation of the bullish influencer is to knock down one wall after another, the temptation of more passive people is to dawdle and procrastinate in the name of waiting for the Spirit of God. Following God's way is not the leisurely way; it is harder work than the bullish way" (Mel Lawrenze, *Spiritual Influence*, p. 89).

- Addressing Acts 14:12-13, Jim Probst notes, "Paul and Barnabas had been on the front-lines of the miraculous. They had even been mistaken for gods (vs. 12-13), and the people sought to offer sacrifices to them! Yet, Paul and Barnabas knew there was only One who had 'opened the doors.'"

DISCUSSION:

1. Select one of the "Discussion Starters" above and share your response with one another.?

2. Ask someone to begin this study by leading the group in prayer.

3. Watch the video segment for week six entitled "Open Doors."

4. Re-state any significant points that you heard in the video teaching today.

5. Read the first "sound bite" for this study. Does your dependence on the Holy Spirit's work cause more comfort or more stress in your life? Explain.

6. Review the "Key Word Study" for this week. What would it look like if the Holy Spirit left your church or your personal ministry? Would anything be different? Explain.

7. "The word 'opportunity' comes from two roots in Latin: *ob* (toward), and *portus* (port of harbor). Opportunity means coming into harbor. That place that is seasonable, suitable, and fit ... When we see the right opportunity before us and set our direction toward it, it is like steering our ship home" (Mel Lawrenze, *Spiritual Influence*, p. 90). Describe a time when you sensed you were "coming into harbor" by following the Holy Spirit's lead.

8. As a group, read Acts 14:8-18. Additionally, read the fourth "sound bite" to further discussion about the Holy Spirit's work and our dependence upon Him.

9. In Friday's daily reading this week, we note that there are four key questions to help discern whether "open doors" are a God-ordained opportunity or a distraction:

10. Is the opportunity consistent with your sense of calling?

11. Is this opportunity God's way of redirecting your calling, purposes, or objectives?

12. Does this opportunity align with biblical values?

13. If the opportunity requires the movement of others, is God moving them as well? (For more insight, read the entire section). Are there other questions or considerations as you evaluate the "open doors" before you?

14. Read Acts 4:29,31; Colossians 4:3-4; 2 Corinthians 2:12; Acts 14:27; Revelation 3:8, 20 to gain a more thorough understanding of "open doors" in Scripture.

15. In light of this *OPEN* study, is there an "open door" that you recognize but have yet to enter? What is holding you back? How can we help?

16. Pray together as a group, asking the Lord to give you courage as you walk through "open doors" this week.

BETWEEN THE MEETINGS:

1) Continue to pray for opportunities to share your story and THE story.

2) Decide on the "next steps" for your personal evangelism. How can you be better prepared and available to share the Good News?

3) Memorize and meditate on Colossians 4:3-4 (see Saturday's daily reading).

4) Continue to discuss the next steps in your small group. What will you study next? How will you demonstrate a "dangerous witness" individually and as a group?

5) Contact a group member to follow up on the prayer requests you've shared this week

CONCLUSION

Thanks for traveling through this study with us. We can boil it down to a two word application: stay open. So please go back and review your personal applications and remain attentive to how the Holy Spirit is leading you into Divine appointments to share your story and the story of our Savior. He specializes in opening doors. We pray "that God may open to us a door for the Word, to declare the mystery of Christ…" (Colossians 4:3).

APPENDIX
JESUS' APOSTLES: THE REST OF THE STORY

We have already explored the life of Peter in an earlier chapter of this book. Some of us, though, would like to know what happened to the other apostles. Here is a brief summary. May each life challenge us toward a ridiculous love and a dangerous witness for Christ.

Andrew, the brother of Peter, is quite a contrast in servant leadership. He was the one who found his brother and brought him to Jesus (John 1:41-42). He was the first one to follow Jesus, but he is never mentioned first. This relatively unknown apostle is only mentioned two more times in Scripture (John 6:8-9 and 12:20-22). Tradition says that he took the message of Christ to Greece and specifically preached in the Province of Achaia. There he was crucified on an X-shaped cross. I'm drawn to his peaceful and dangerous witness.

James son of Zebedee, a guy who particularly seemed marked by ambition, was one of the three significant disciples that made up the

intimate inner circle of Jesus', along with Peter and John. There is
one significant passage that reveals James' true identity. This disciple who had witnessed the transfiguration and the intimate prayer
time in the Garden of Gethsemane was the one who stood strong to
the end and witnessed to the resurrected Christ and paid for it with
his life (Acts 12:1-2). He is the only apostle whose story of martyrdom is recorded in the New Testament. We don't know the specifics.
We only know that King Herod had James put to death by the sword.
At his death he fulfills the prophetic words of Jesus, "You will drink
the cup I drink and be baptized with the baptism I am baptized
with…" (Mark 10:39). Ambition properly channeled glorifies our
Lord.

John, the disciple whom Jesus loved (John 19:26; 20:2; 21:7; and
21:20), has an extraordinary story to tell, younger brother to James,
a second child of Zebedee and Salome. He had such significant influence in the life of the early church that the Apostle Paul makes a
passing comment of him in Galatians 2:9, "James, Peter, and John,
those reputed to be pillars, gave me and Barnabas the right hand of
fellowship when they recognized the grace given to me."

It is well-documented John spent his last years in and around
Ephesus. He probably wrote his Gospel and his letters from that location. Three significant church leaders were discipled by John:

Polycarp, Papias, and Ignatius. Eventually his preaching and disciple-making prompted the Emperor Domitian to banish John to Patmos, an island that housed political prisoners just off the southeast coast of Asia or modern day Turkey. It was in that location he wrote Revelation. He was eventually set free by Emperor Nerva in 96 AD and returned to the city of Ephesus. Church tradition says that he lived to be quite old. He was no longer able to walk on his own and so John was carried to the various house churches that were used as places of worship. His abiding theme and constant instruction was the same, "Little children, love one another." John, the last living apostle, died of natural causes.

Philip, the down-to-earth disciple is mentioned four times in the Gospels (John 1:43-45; 6:5-7; 12:20-22; and 14:8). The most significant shaping of Philip is located in the Upper Room where he speaks these regrettable words, "Lord, show us the Father and that will be enough for us" (John 14:8). For three plus years Jesus had revealed his divine connection to the Father. Miracle after miracle, teaching after teaching, day after day, Jesus had given evidence of his intimate relationship with God. Philip had looked into the face of God over and over again and yet, somehow had missed Him. The Good News is that ultimately Philip did recognize in Jesus the God of the universe. Tradition tells us that he preached throughout the Roman provinces of Galatia and Phrygia. The sketchy testimony is that Philip was put to death by stoning at Heliopolis in Phrygia some eight years after James was killed in Jerusalem, but not before he brought many to Jesus.

Nathanael, friend of Philip, straight-shooter, and sometimes called Bartholomew, is our sixth apostle. He is only mentioned twice in John's Gospel (John 1:45-51 and 21:2). We don't know how he died for his faith in Jesus. Three primary theories emerge. Early church tradition indicated that Nathanael preached through Persia and India. One theory says he was tied up in a sack and thrown in the sea. Another says he was flayed to death with sharp knives! The final view declares that he was crucified. Regardless, the evidence seems to point to a martyr's death.

Thomas, the guy who is eternally labeled as a doubter, is our seventh apostle. The words that have been used to describe this disciple include worrywart, pessimistic, melancholy, dark, brooding, and sullen. Yikes! On three separate occasions he speaks in John's Gospel (11:26; 14:5; and 20:25-28). Tradition tells us that Thomas carried the Gospel to India or perhaps Persia. There is a monument in southern India that marks his coming. Thomas was martyred for his faith in Jesus by being either shot through with arrows or run through with a spear while praying.

Matthew or Levi, the transformed tax-collector, is our eighth apostle. It was at a Roman toll booth for tax collecting that Matthew was called by Jesus into a life of apprenticeship (Matthew 9:9 and Luke 5:29-32). Beyond this we don't know a great deal about his biography. It appears that he ministered for a long time throughout Palestine and the larger region winning other Jews to Christ. The earliest records indicate that he was burned at the stake. Some suggest that he was killed by the sword in Ethiopia. The converted internal revenue service agent gave up his potential life of great wealth and luxury in order to make eternal investments in God's larger Kingdom.

James son of Alphaeus is our ninth apostle, sometimes referred to as James the Less or James the Unknown (Mark 15:40). This tiny piece of information could possibly be a reference to his small physical size or perhaps to his young age. The only mention of him, besides the Mark reference, is his name being listed among the other apostles. That's it! He sought no recognition and never uttered a recorded syllable. Somehow by God's overwhelming grace he became a preacher of the Good News. Tradition says that he carried the Gospel to Syria and Persia. Others claim that he went to Spain and on to Britain. Confusion over his death remains as well. Some records indicate that he was stoned to death. Others declare that he was beaten to death, while still others say that he was crucified. In the end, James the Less, carried on the ministry of Jesus in obscurity, except in the eyes of eternity.

Thaddaeus, also called Judas, the brother of James, is the tenth man called by Jesus to be His disciple. Like so many of these early apprentices of Jesus, we know next to nothing about him. He speaks once in John's Gospel in the Upper Room discourse by asking this question of Jesus, "But, Lord, why do you intend to show yourself to us and not to the world?" (John 14:22). After those dramatic days in Jerusalem he spent the rest of his life articulating the Good News of Jesus resurrection. He apparently traveled north to Edessa, modern day Turkey, healing, preaching, and loving in the Name of Jesus. Tradition tells us he was clubbed to death for the Savior.

Simon the Zealot, the fiery anti-Roman-government disciple, is always somehow paired with the most liberal thinking apostle and the only non-Galilean, *Judas Iscariot.* What a strange pair (Matthew 10:4 and Mark 3:18)! Originally Simon was a part of an extreme outlaw political sect. These zealots often expressed their hatred of Rome through terrorism. They longed for a political Messiah who would overthrow Roman oppression and restore God's rule over Israel. Zealots often carried concealed daggers in their robes and were referred to as "sicarii" or "dagger men." stealthily slipping up on a

Roman politician, an occupying soldier, or a government sympathizer and slitting their throat. Gruesome! The love of Jesus somehow worked its way into the very depths of this man and he was forever changed.

Judas Iscariot on the other hand, the keeper of the money purse, the embezzler of funds, and the ultimate betrayer, was a complete opposite to Simon. (John 12:1-6). He complained of excess and waste (John 12:4-5). Perhaps, like Simon, he had hoped for a political Messiah. He sold out for thirty pieces of silver (Matthew 26:14-16). All four Gospels tell us his betrayal. His remorse was never repentance (Matthew 27:3-8 and Acts 1:18-19). He died, not as a martyr, but as a man who completely missed the unfathomable love of Christ.

Matthias, the replacement of Judas Iscariot, is our final apostle in this brief portrait. Acts 1:12-26 tells us of his selection by the Holy Spirit in the life of the early church. He is nowhere mentioned in the New Testament, except in his appointment as one who had seen Jesus and subsequently called to witness to the resurrection of Jesus. Tradition says that he was first stoned and then beheaded with an ax because of his abiding love and testimony to Jesus as Lord and Savior.

WORKS CITED

Bennett, A.G. (1975). *The Valley of Vision: A Collection of Puritan Prayers and Devotions.* Carlisle: Banner of Truth.

Chambers, A. (2009). *Eats with Sinners.* Cincinnati: Standard Publishing Company.

Drobner, H.R., & W. Harmless. Eds. (2007). The Acts of the Scillitan Martyrs. In *The Fathers of the Church: A Comprehensive Introduction.* (pp.). Peabody: Hendrickson Publishers.

Hunter, G. (2003). *Radical Outreach: Recovery of Apostolic Ministry and Evangelism.* Nashville: Abingdon Press.

Hybels, B. (2006). *Just Walk Across the Room.* Grand Rapids: Zondervan.

Lawrence, M. (2012). *Spiritual Influence: The Hidden Power Behind Leadership.* Grand Rapids: Zondervan.

Metaxas, E. (2010). *Bonhoeffer: Pastor, Martyr, Prophet, Spy.* Nashville: Thomas Nelson.

Patton, M. (2004). *Should Christians Have Unbelieving Friends?* Retrieved March 1, 2014, from Bible.org/article/should-Christians-have-unbelieving-friends

Shepherd, D.R. (Ed.) (1998). *The Writings of Justin Martyr.* Nashville: Broadman & Holman.

Sweet, L. (1999). *Aqua Church: Essential Leadership Arts for Piloting Your Church in Today's Fluid Culture.* Colorado Springs: David C. Cook.

Swindoll, C.R. (1998). *The Tale of the Tardy Oxcart.* Nashville: Thomas Nelson.

Warren, R. (2009). *The Purpose Driven Life.* Grand Rapids: Zondervan.

White, J. (1976). *The Cost of Commitment.* Downers Grove: Inter-Varsity Press.

ABOUT THE AUTHORS

This book represents just a portion of the entire "Open" all-church study for Eastview Christian Church. The authors for this project have invested countless hours in prayer, preparation and presentation of this material. I count it a remarkable privilege and honor to live out these concepts with such a dedicated team of servant leaders. For more information about the authors and ministries, visit our website at www.eastviewchurch.net.

Mike Baker	Senior Pastor
Tyler Hari	Pastor of Outreach
J.K. Jones, Jr.	Pastor of Spiritual Formation
Jim Probst	Pastor of Small Groups

Special Thanks:

Thank you to all of the hard-working and creative individuals who have helped to create not only the "Open" book, but the videos and small group discussions for this series! As always, a project of this magnitude requires more team members and "behind the scenes help" than can be listed, but here's a great start; thank you to Karen Norris and Alyssa Deffner for their tireless creative energy in developing the artwork and concepts for the book and videos that truly amaze me. Thanks also to Scott Sarver and Shawn Prokes for their video expertise! Thank you also to Julie Pond for her copy editing and formatting even in the midst of moving across the country! And a HUGE thank you to the Eastview congregation members who already live Open lives and have so readily shared their stories to make the book come alive! And finally, thank you to Mike Baker, J.K. Jones and Tyler Hari for their oversight and depth of knowledge in the historical and cross-cultural examples that serve as awesome illustrations in this book. I am truly blessed to be surrounded by people with OPEN lives for Christ!

In Christ,
Jim Probst

Mahipau – Week One (Wednesday)

Rosie Archer – Week One
(Thursday)

Sanjay – Week Two (Wednesday)

Mark Hapke – Week Two
(Thursday)

Pastor Benyu – Week Three
(Wednesday)

John Ashenfelter – Week Three
(Thursday)

Diwas – Week Four
(Wednesday)

Jessica Bockman – Week Four
(Thursday)

Tiharu – Week Five (Wednesday)

Wayne Stewart – Week
Five (Thursday)

Sarat – Week Six (Wednesday)

Connie Urosevich –
Week Six (Thursday)

OTHER STUDIES AVAILABLE

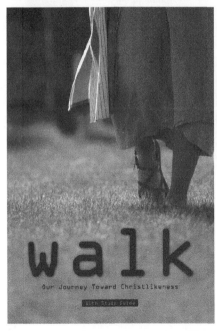

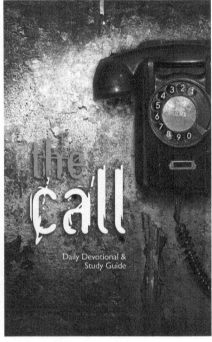

To order:
www.eastviewchurch.net
Harvest Book Store 309-451-5001